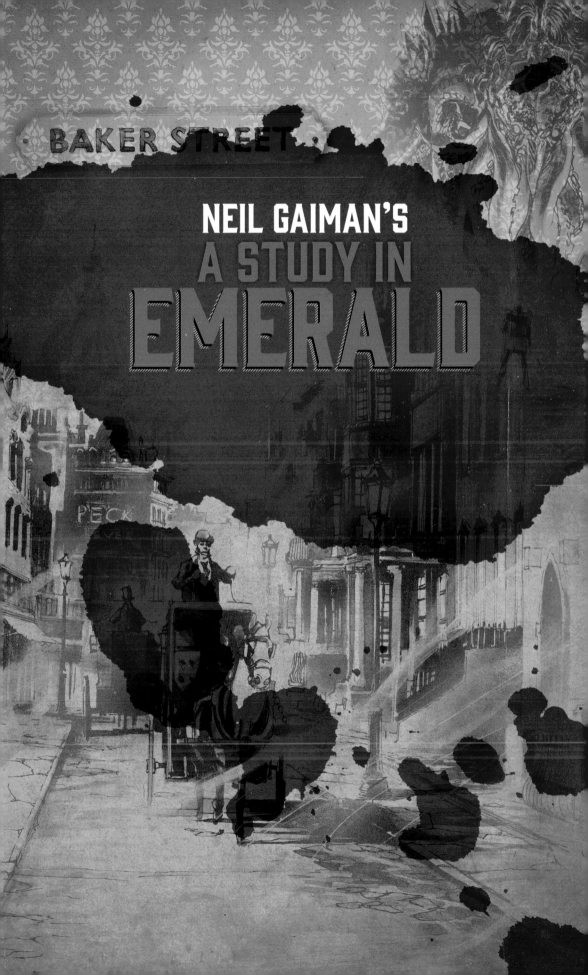

BAKER STREET

NEIL GAIMAN'S
A STUDY IN
EMERALD

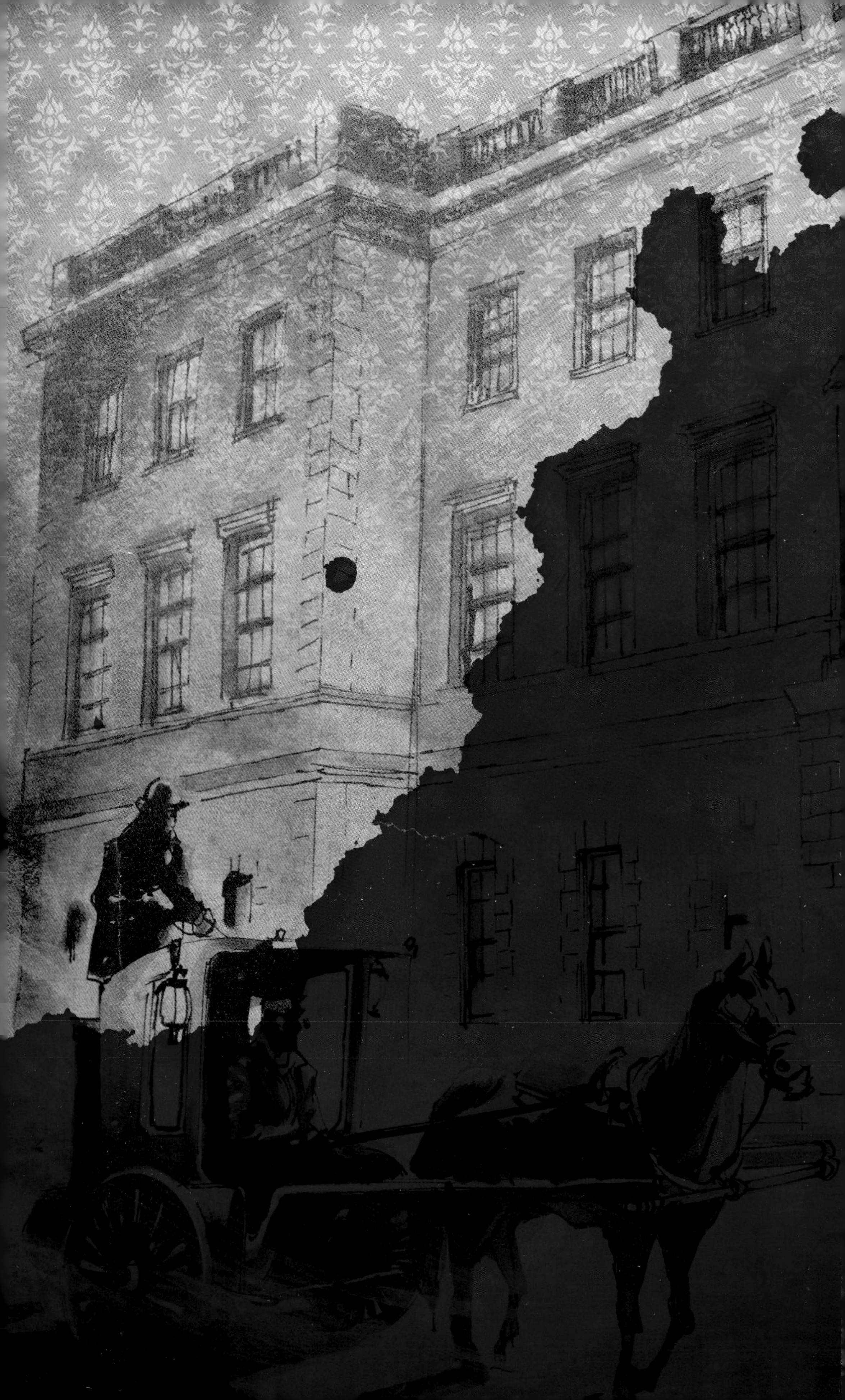

A STUDY IN EMERALD

Story and words
NEIL GAIMAN

Art and adaptation script
RAFAEL ALBUQUERQUE

Adaptation script
RAFAEL SCAVONE

Colors
DAVE STEWART

Letters
TODD KLEIN

DARK HORSE BOOKS

president and publisher
MIKE RICHARDSON

editor
DANIEL CHABON

assistant editor
BRETT ISRAEL

designer
ANITA MAGAÑA

digital art technician
CHRISTIANNE GOUDREAU

Published by Dark Horse Books
A division of Dark Horse Comics, Inc.
10956 SE Main Street | Milwaukie, OR 97222
DarkHorse.com
To find a comic shop in your area,
check out the Comic Shop Locator Service: comicshoplocator.com

First edition: June 2018
ISBN 978-1-50670-393-0
10 9 8 7 6 5 4 3 2 1
Printed in China

Names: Gaiman, Neil, author. | Albuquerque, Rafael, 1981- artist, author. |
  Scavone, Rafael, author. | Stewart, Dave, colourist. | Klein, Todd,
  letterer.
Title: A study in emerald / Neil Gaiman, story and words ; Rafael
  Albuquerque, art and adaptation script ; Rafael Scavone, adaptation script
  ; Dave Stewart, colors ; Todd Klein, letters.
Other titles: At head of title: Neil Gaiman's
Description: First edition. | Milwaukie, OR : Dark Horse Books, 2018.
Identifiers: LCCN 2017061474 | ISBN 9781506703930 (hardback)
Subjects: LCSH: Graphic novels. | BISAC: COMICS & GRAPHIC NOVELS / Science
  Fiction. | COMICS & GRAPHIC NOVELS / Crime & Mystery. | COMICS & GRAPHIC
  NOVELS / General.
Classification: LCC PN6737.G3 S78 2018 | DDC 741.5/942--dc23
LC record available at https://lccn.loc.gov/2017061474

THE NEW FRIEND

THE STRAND PLAYERS

PRESENTS

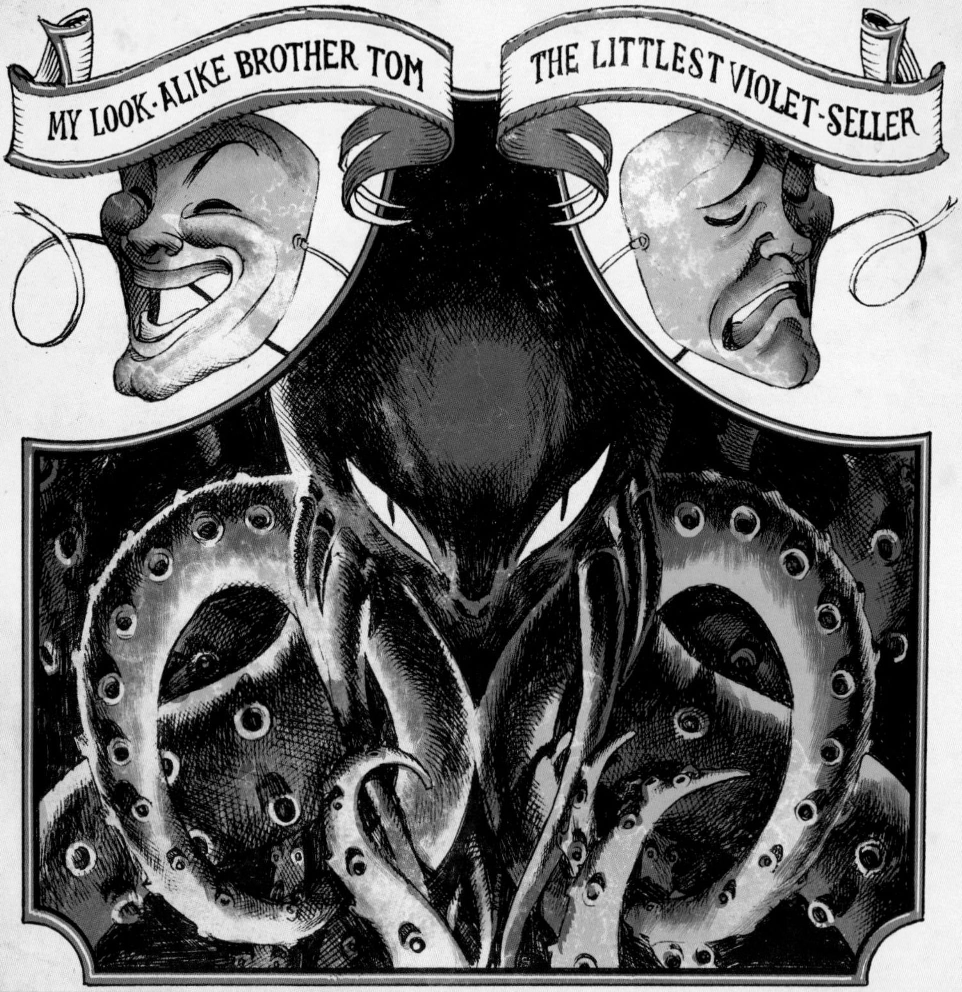
MY LOOK-ALIKE BROTHER TOM
THE LITTLEST VIOLET-SELLER

THE GREAT OLD ONES COME

Fresh from Their Stupendous European Tour, where they performed before several of the **CROWNED HEADS OF EUROPE**, garnering their **plaudits** and **praise** with **magnificent dramatic performances**, combining both **COMEDY** and **TRAGEDY**, the **Strand Players** wish to make it known that they shall be appearing at the **Royal Court Theatre, Drury Lane**, for a **LIMITED ENGAGEMENT** in April, at which they will present *"My Look-Alike Brother Tom!" "The Littlest Violet-Seller"* and *"The Great Old Ones Come,"* (this last an Historical Epic of Pageantry and Delight); each an entire play in one act!

Tickets are available now from the Box Office.

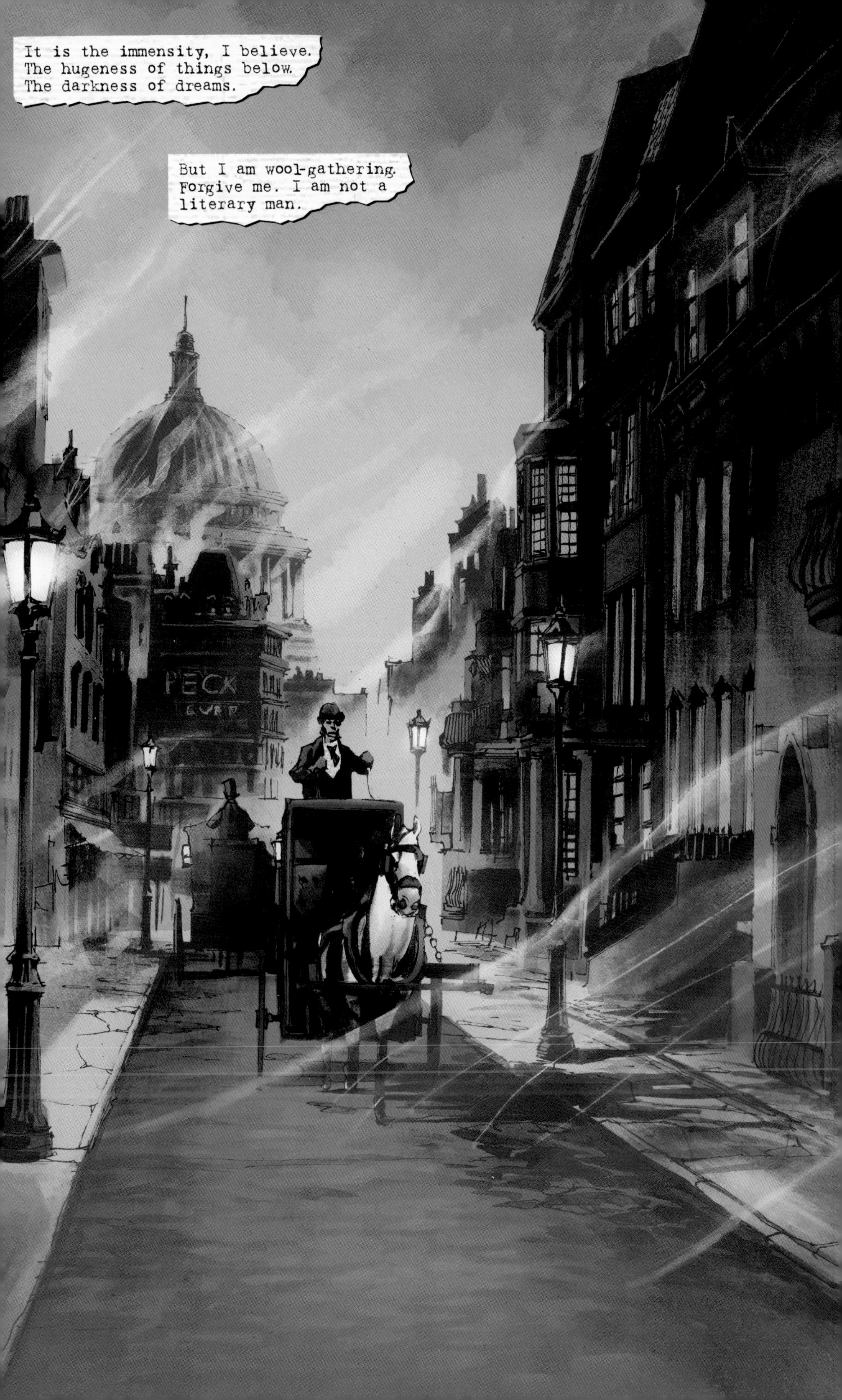
It is the immensity, I believe. The hugeness of things below. The darkness of dreams.
But I am wool-gathering. Forgive me. I am not a literary man.
PECK

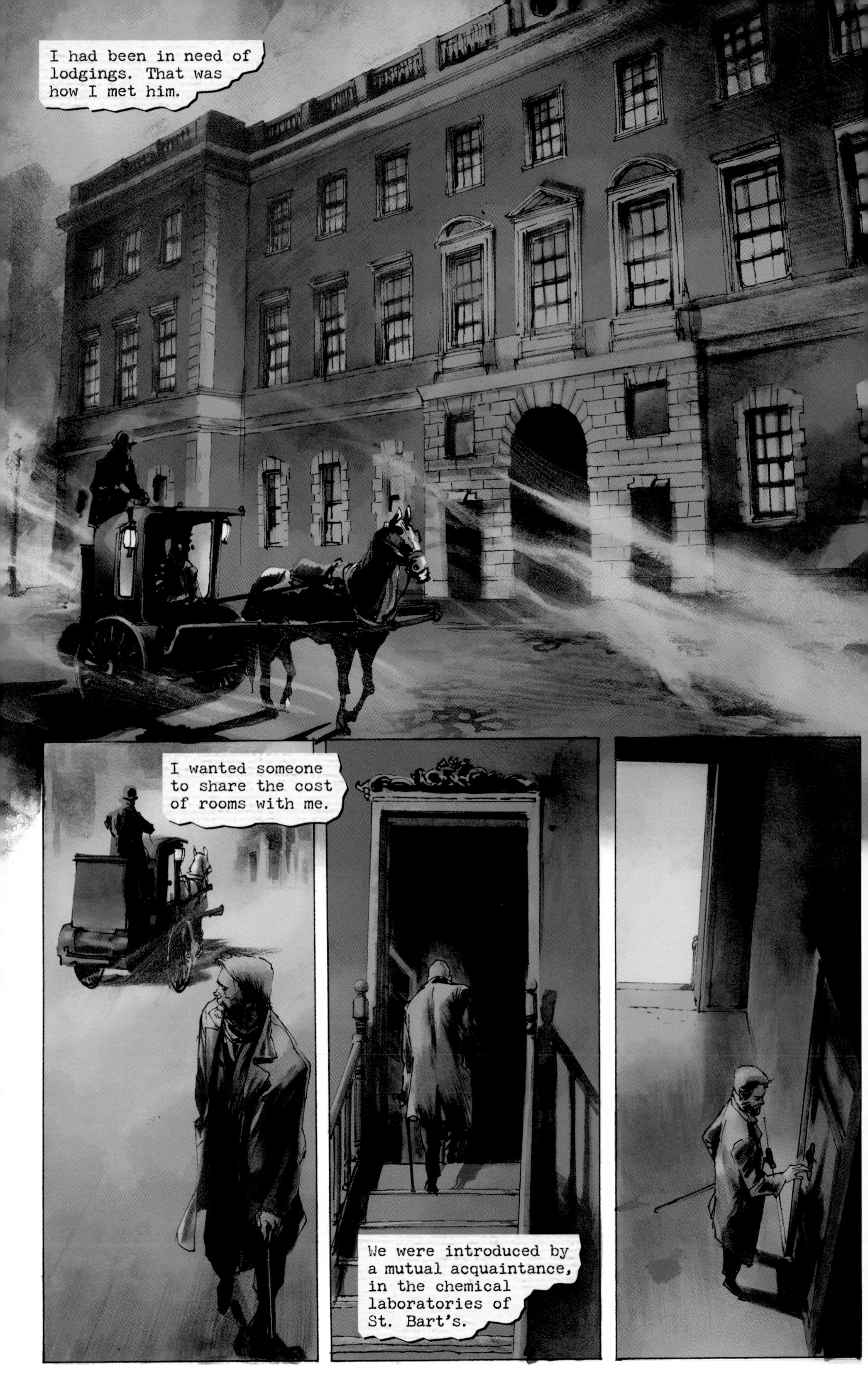
I had been in need of lodgings. That was how I met him.
I wanted someone to share the cost of rooms with me.
We were introduced by a mutual acquaintance, in the chemical laboratories of St. Bart's.

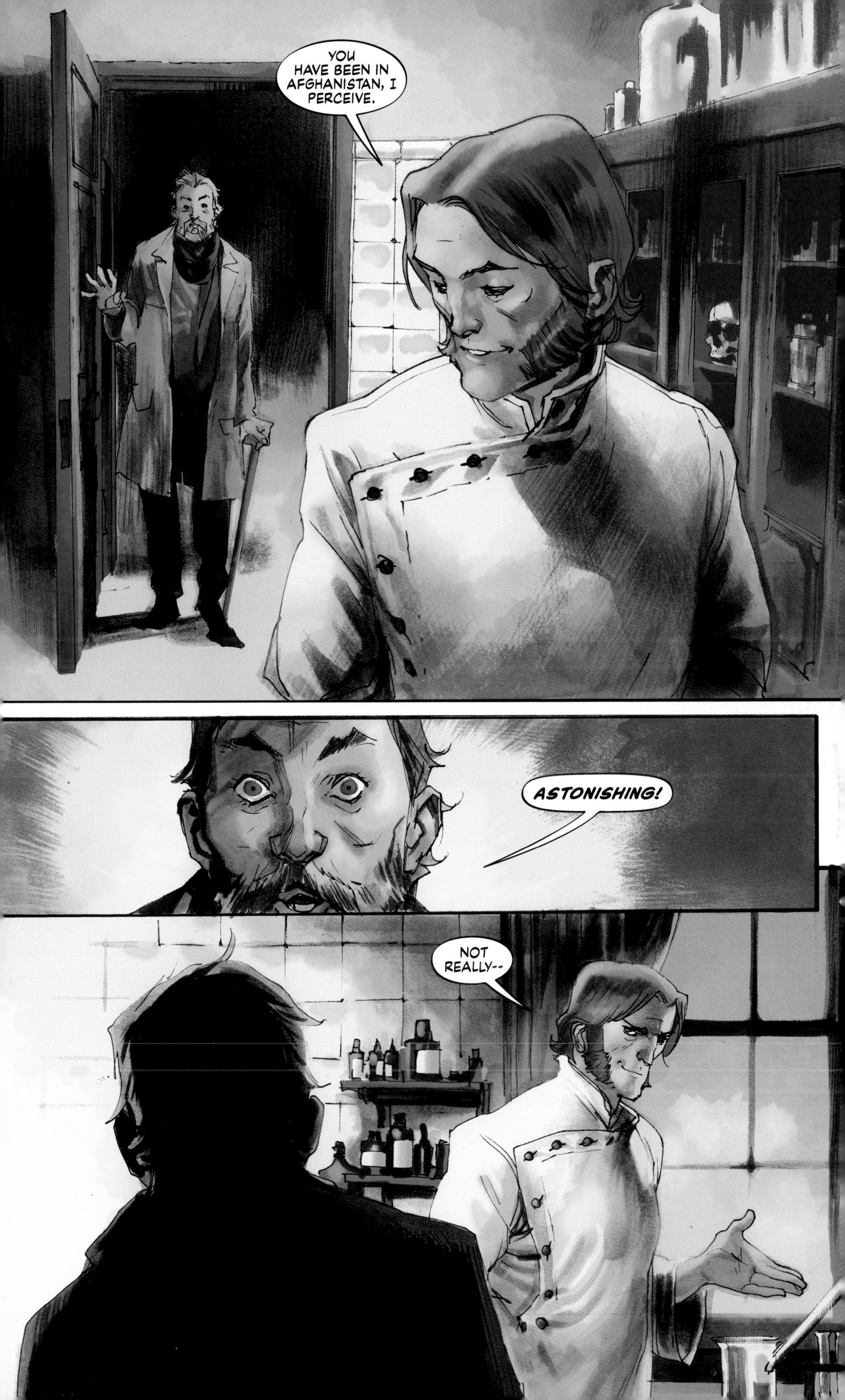
YOU HAVE BEEN IN AFGHANISTAN, I PERCEIVE.
ASTONISHING!
NOT REALLY--

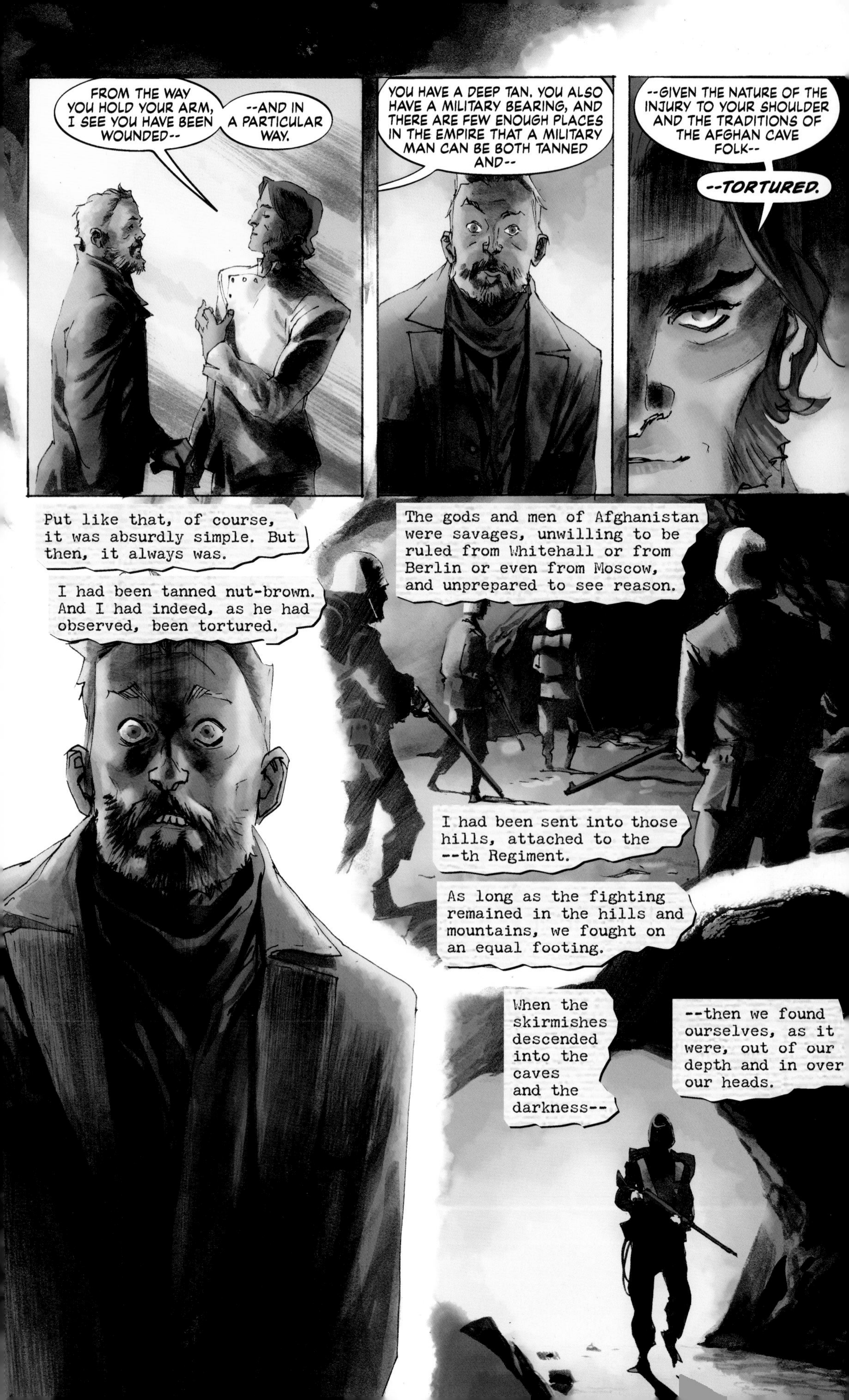
FROM THE WAY YOU HOLD YOUR ARM, I SEE YOU HAVE BEEN WOUNDED--
--AND IN A PARTICULAR WAY.
YOU HAVE A DEEP TAN. YOU ALSO HAVE A MILITARY BEARING, AND THERE ARE FEW ENOUGH PLACES IN THE EMPIRE THAT A MILITARY MAN CAN BE BOTH TANNED AND--
--GIVEN THE NATURE OF THE INJURY TO YOUR SHOULDER AND THE TRADITIONS OF THE AFGHAN CAVE FOLK--
--TORTURED.
Put like that, of course, it was absurdly simple. But then, it always was.
I had been tanned nut-brown. And I had indeed, as he had observed, been tortured.
The gods and men of Afghanistan were savages, unwilling to be ruled from Whitehall or from Berlin or even from Moscow, and unprepared to see reason.
I had been sent into those hills, attached to the --th Regiment.
As long as the fighting remained in the hills and mountains, we fought on an equal footing.
When the skirmishes descended into the caves and the darkness--
--then we found ourselves, as it were, out of our depth and in over our heads.

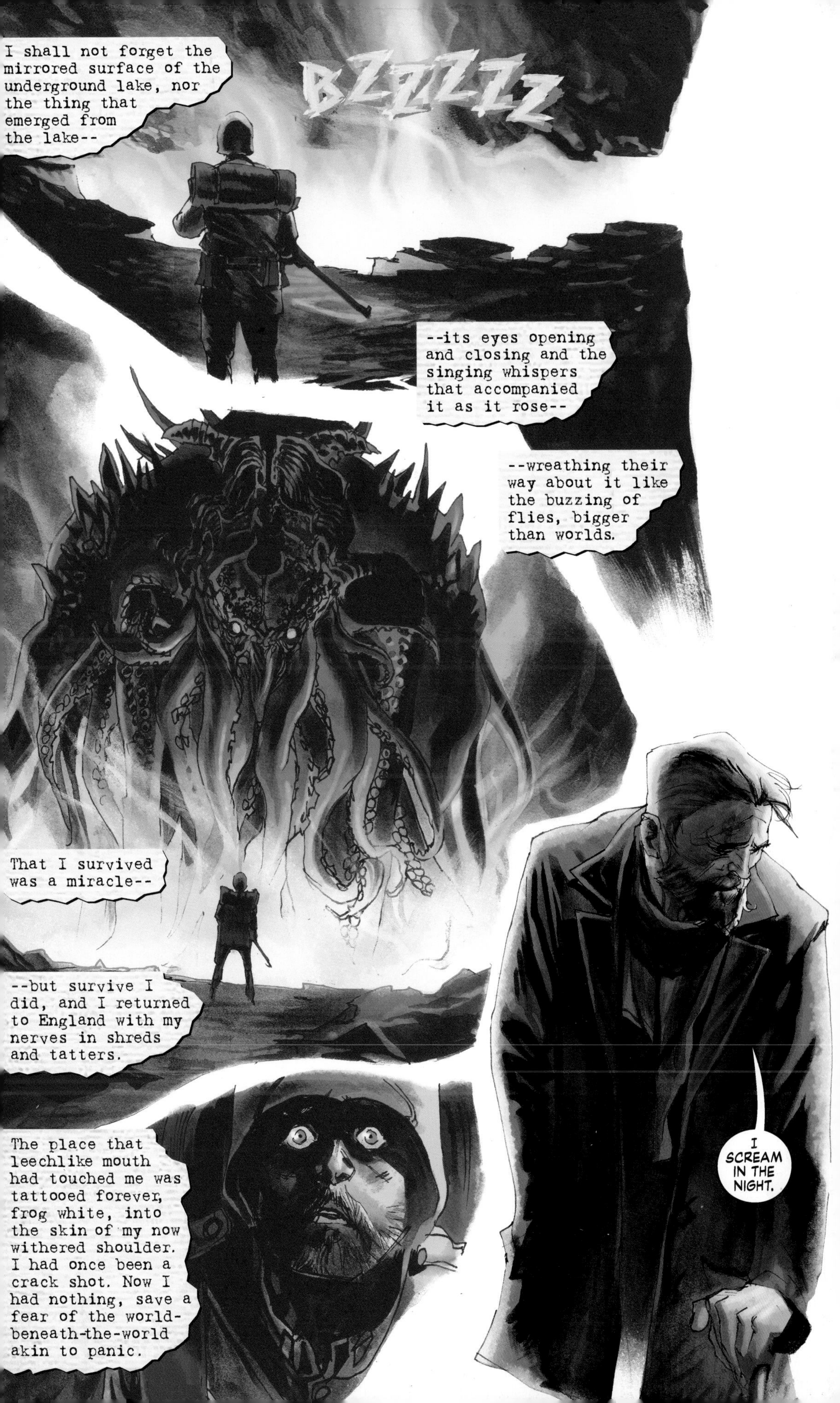
I shall not forget the mirrored surface of the underground lake, nor the thing that emerged from the lake--
BZZZZZ
--its eyes opening and closing and the singing whispers that accompanied it as it rose--
--wreathing their way about it like the buzzing of flies, bigger than worlds.
That I survived was a miracle--
--but survive I did, and I returned to England with my nerves in shreds and tatters.
The place that leechlike mouth had touched me was tattooed forever, frog white, into the skin of my now withered shoulder. I had once been a crack shot. Now I had nothing, save a fear of the world-beneath-the-world akin to panic.
I SCREAM IN THE NIGHT.

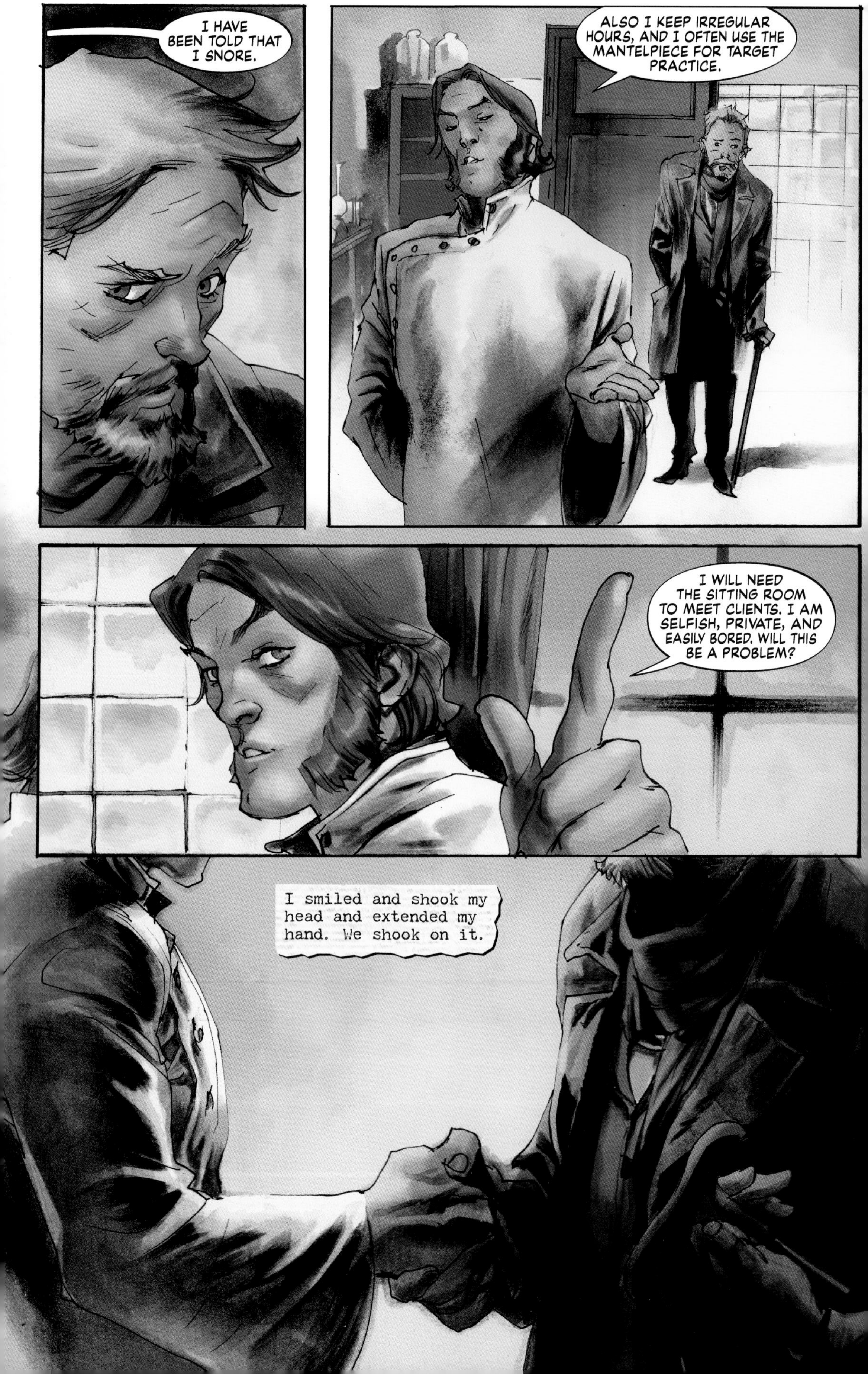
I HAVE BEEN TOLD THAT I SNORE.
ALSO I KEEP IRREGULAR HOURS, AND I OFTEN USE THE MANTELPIECE FOR TARGET PRACTICE.
I WILL NEED THE SITTING ROOM TO MEET CLIENTS. I AM SELFISH, PRIVATE, AND EASILY BORED. WILL THIS BE A PROBLEM?
I smiled and shook my head and extended my hand. We shook on it.

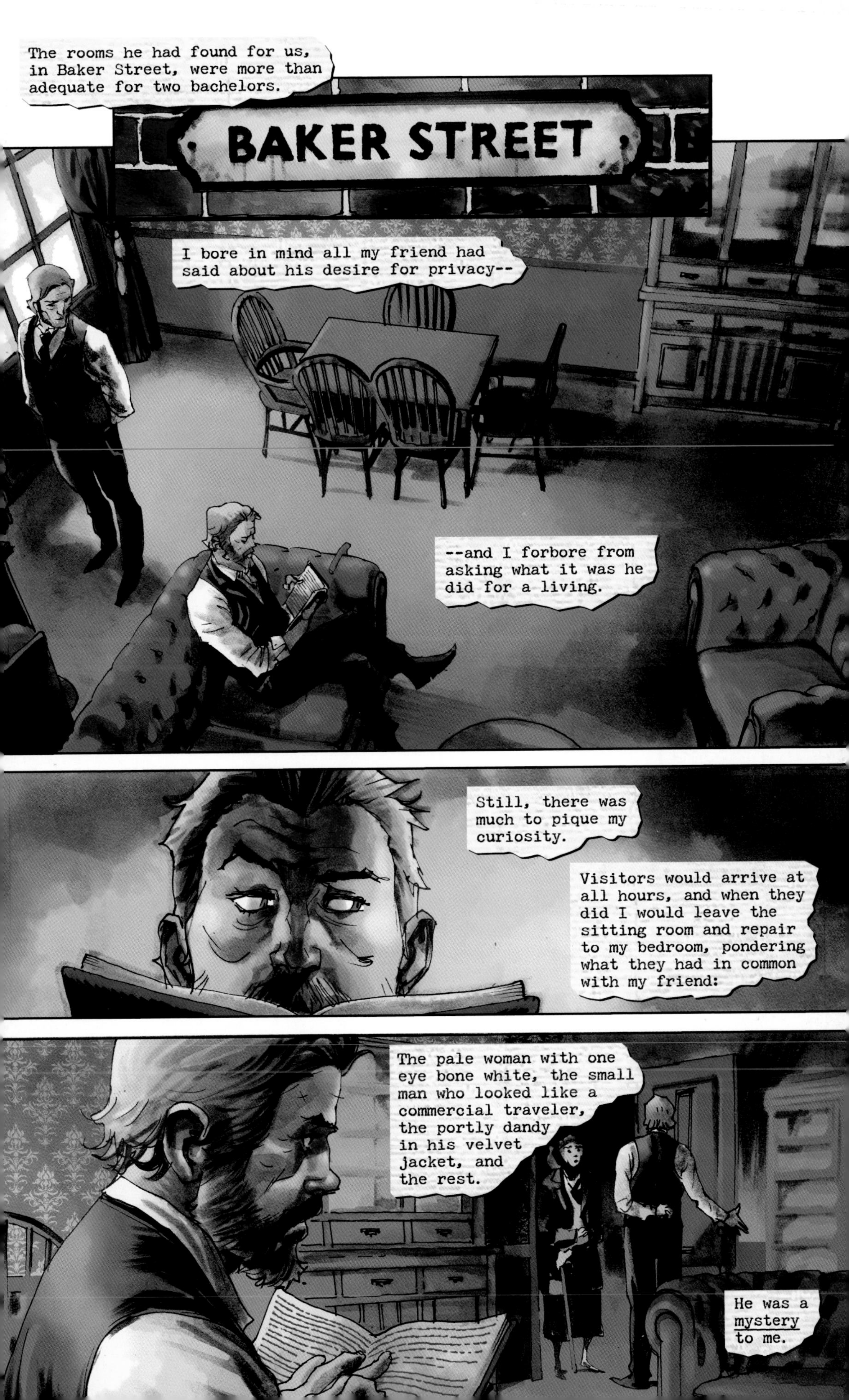
The rooms he had found for us, in Baker Street, were more than adequate for two bachelors.
BAKER STREET
I bore in mind all my friend had said about his desire for privacy--
--and I forbore from asking what it was he did for a living.
Still, there was much to pique my curiosity.
Visitors would arrive at all hours, and when they did I would leave the sitting room and repair to my bedroom, pondering what they had in common with my friend:
The pale woman with one eye bone white, the small man who looked like a commercial traveler, the portly dandy in his velvet jacket, and the rest.
He was a mystery to me.

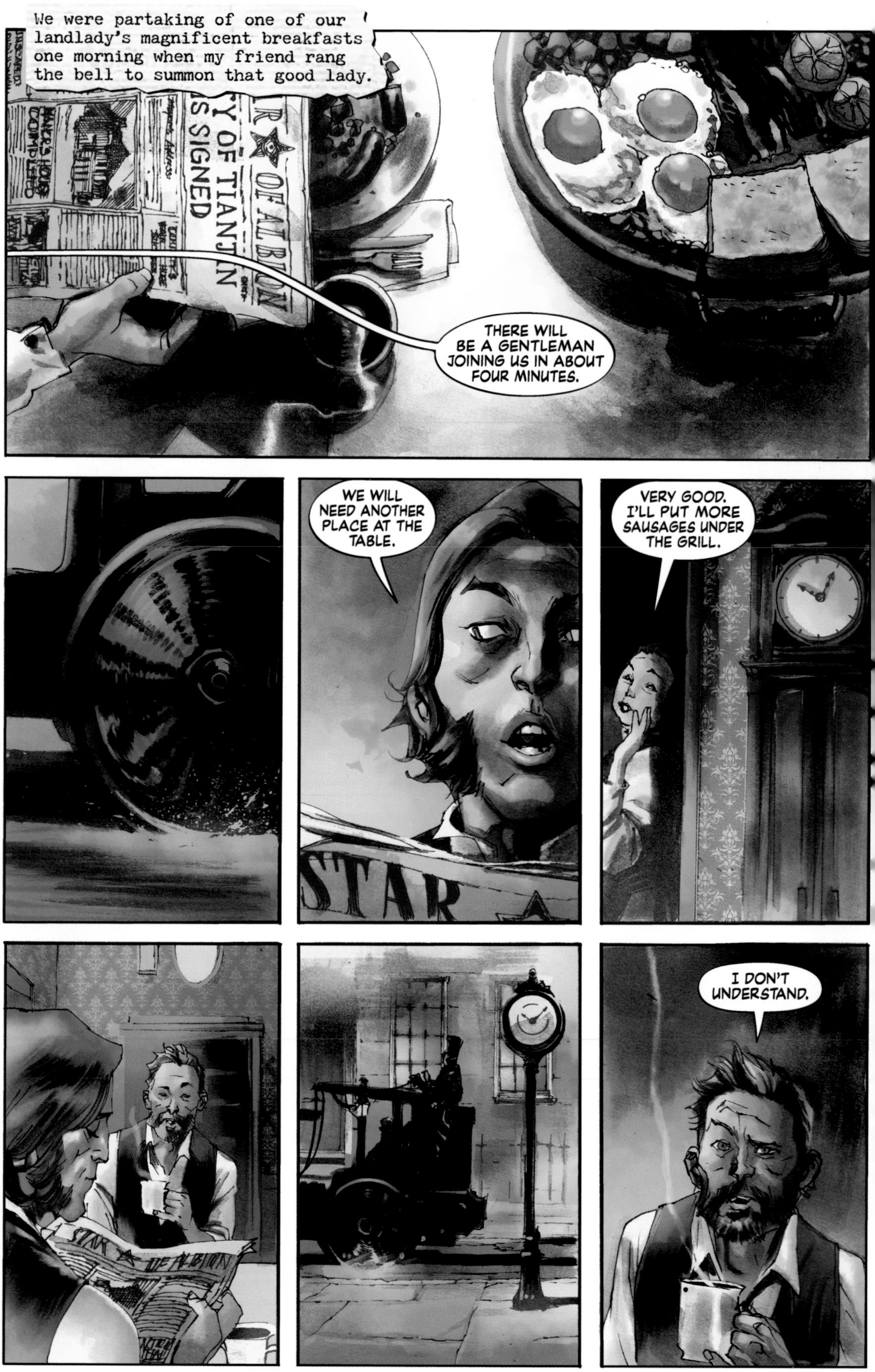

We were partaking of one of our landlady's magnificent breakfasts one morning when my friend rang the bell to summon that good lady.
THERE WILL BE A GENTLEMAN JOINING US IN ABOUT FOUR MINUTES.
WE WILL NEED ANOTHER PLACE AT THE TABLE.
VERY GOOD. I'LL PUT MORE SAUSAGES UNDER THE GRILL.
I DON'T UNDERSTAND.

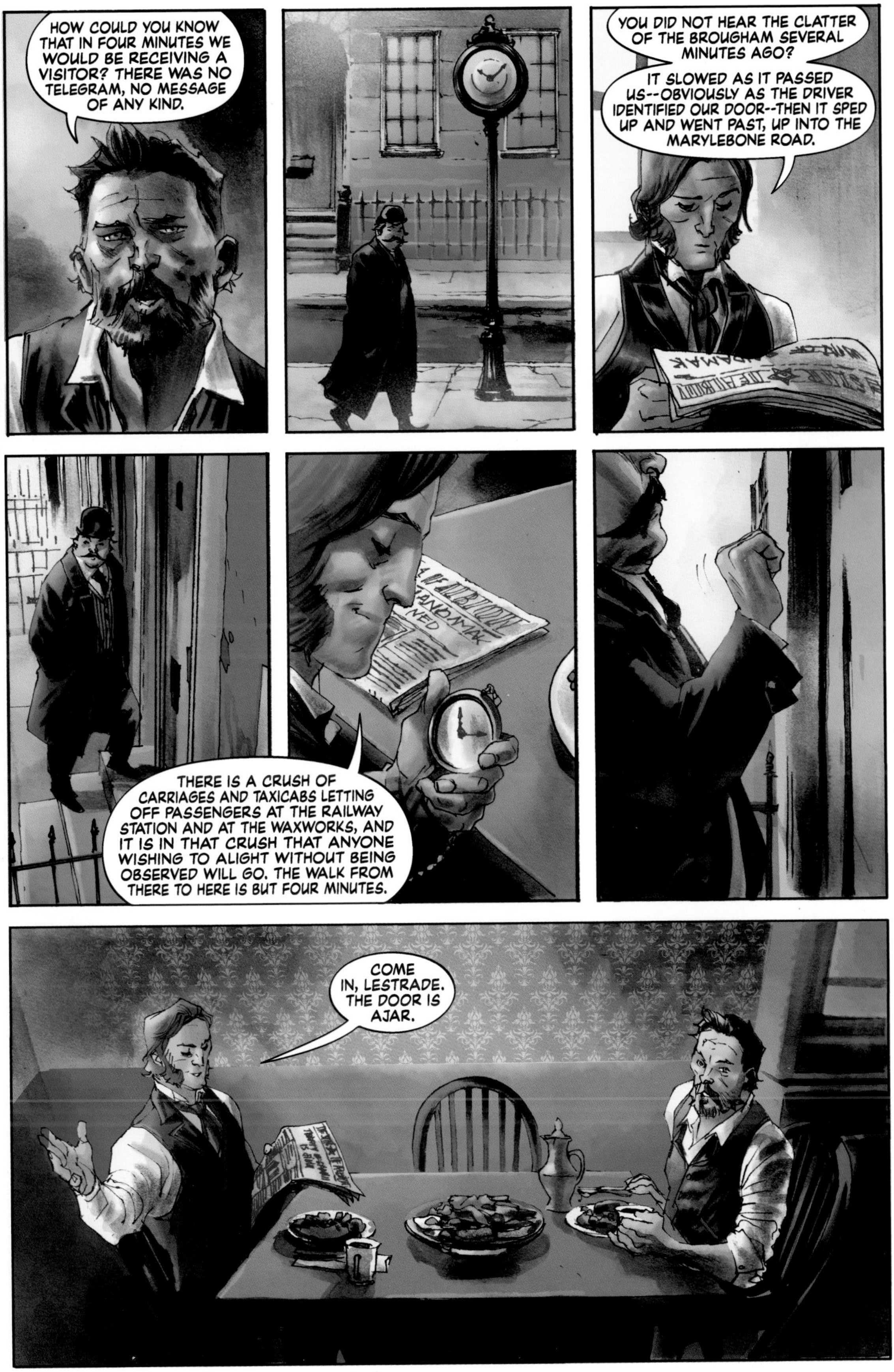
HOW COULD YOU KNOW THAT IN FOUR MINUTES WE WOULD BE RECEIVING A VISITOR? THERE WAS NO TELEGRAM, NO MESSAGE OF ANY KIND.
YOU DID NOT HEAR THE CLATTER OF THE BROUGHAM SEVERAL MINUTES AGO?
IT SLOWED AS IT PASSED US--OBVIOUSLY AS THE DRIVER IDENTIFIED OUR DOOR--THEN IT SPED UP AND WENT PAST, UP INTO THE MARYLEBONE ROAD.
THERE IS A CRUSH OF CARRIAGES AND TAXICABS LETTING OFF PASSENGERS AT THE RAILWAY STATION AND AT THE WAXWORKS, AND IT IS IN THAT CRUSH THAT ANYONE WISHING TO ALIGHT WITHOUT BEING OBSERVED WILL GO. THE WALK FROM THERE TO HERE IS BUT FOUR MINUTES.
COME IN, LESTRADE. THE DOOR IS AJAR.

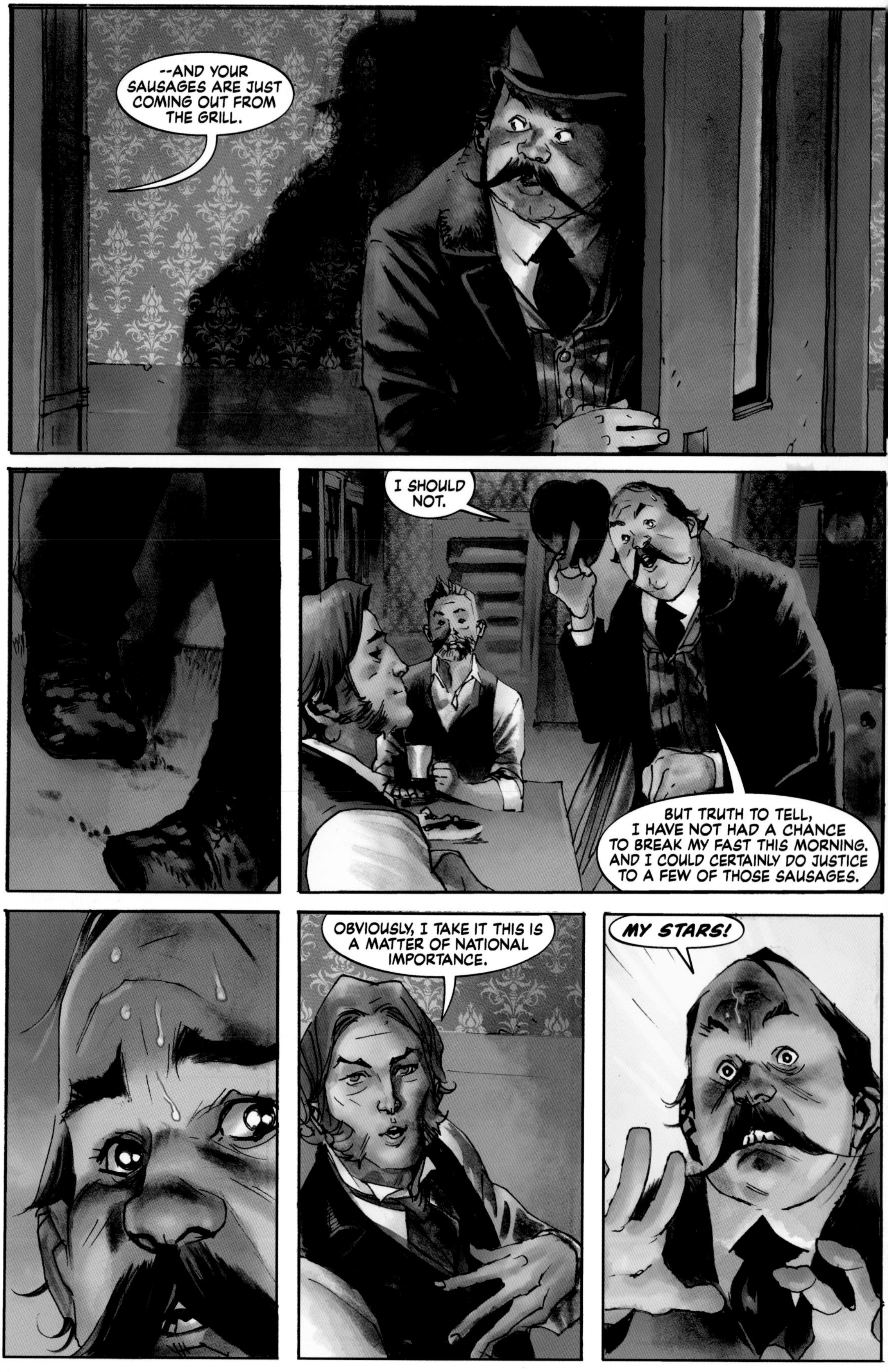
--AND YOUR SAUSAGES ARE JUST COMING OUT FROM THE GRILL.
I SHOULD NOT.
BUT TRUTH TO TELL, I HAVE NOT HAD A CHANCE TO BREAK MY FAST THIS MORNING. AND I COULD CERTAINLY DO JUSTICE TO A FEW OF THOSE SAUSAGES.
OBVIOUSLY, I TAKE IT THIS IS A MATTER OF NATIONAL IMPORTANCE.
MY STARS!

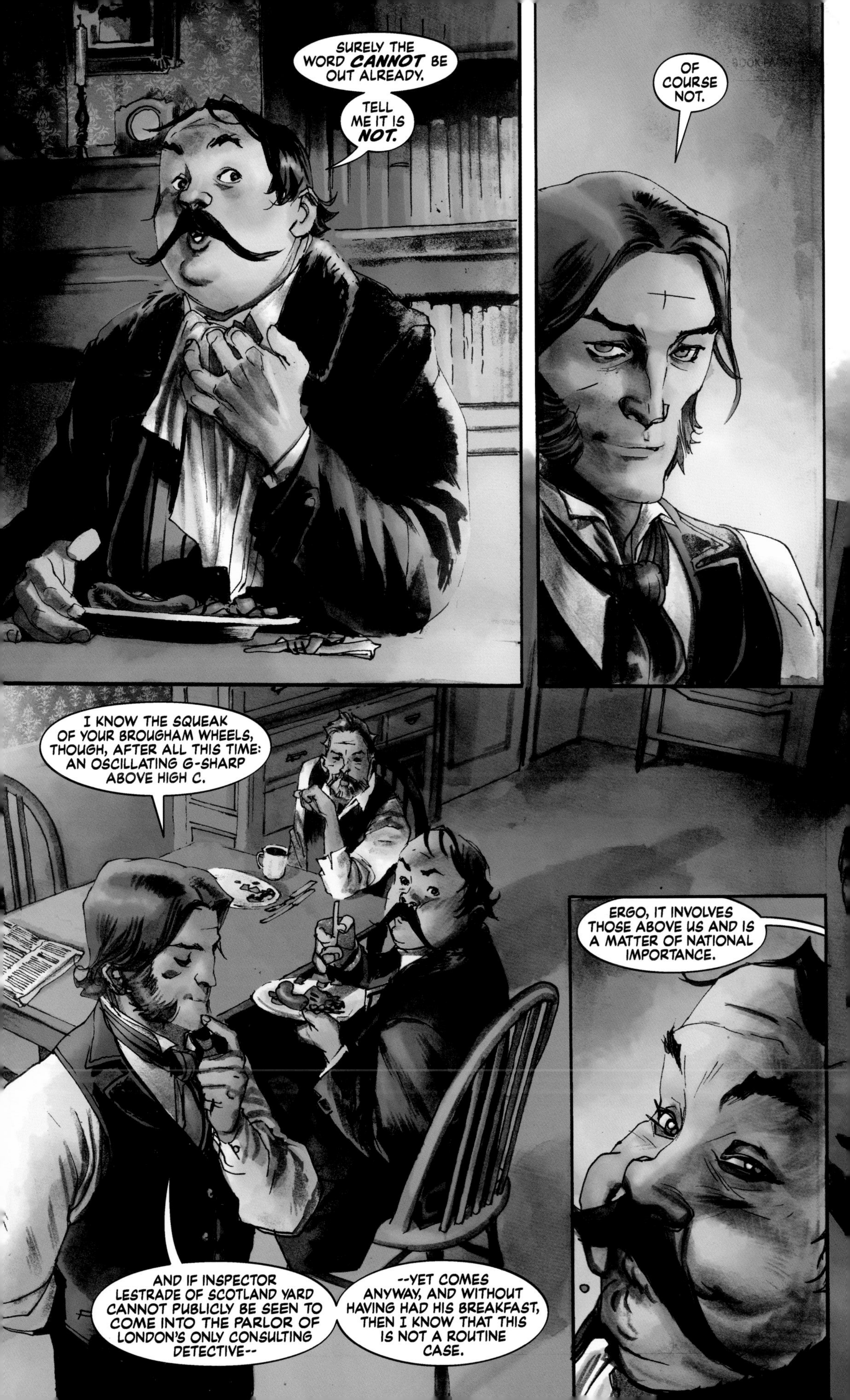
SURELY THE WORD CANNOT BE OUT ALREADY.
TELL ME IT IS NOT.
OF COURSE NOT.
I KNOW THE SQUEAK OF YOUR BROUGHAM WHEELS, THOUGH, AFTER ALL THIS TIME: AN OSCILLATING G-SHARP ABOVE HIGH C.
AND IF INSPECTOR LESTRADE OF SCOTLAND YARD CANNOT PUBLICLY BE SEEN TO COME INTO THE PARLOR OF LONDON'S ONLY CONSULTING DETECTIVE--
--YET COMES ANYWAY, AND WITHOUT HAVING HAD HIS BREAKFAST, THEN I KNOW THAT THIS IS NOT A ROUTINE CASE.
ERGO, IT INVOLVES THOSE ABOVE US AND IS A MATTER OF NATIONAL IMPORTANCE.

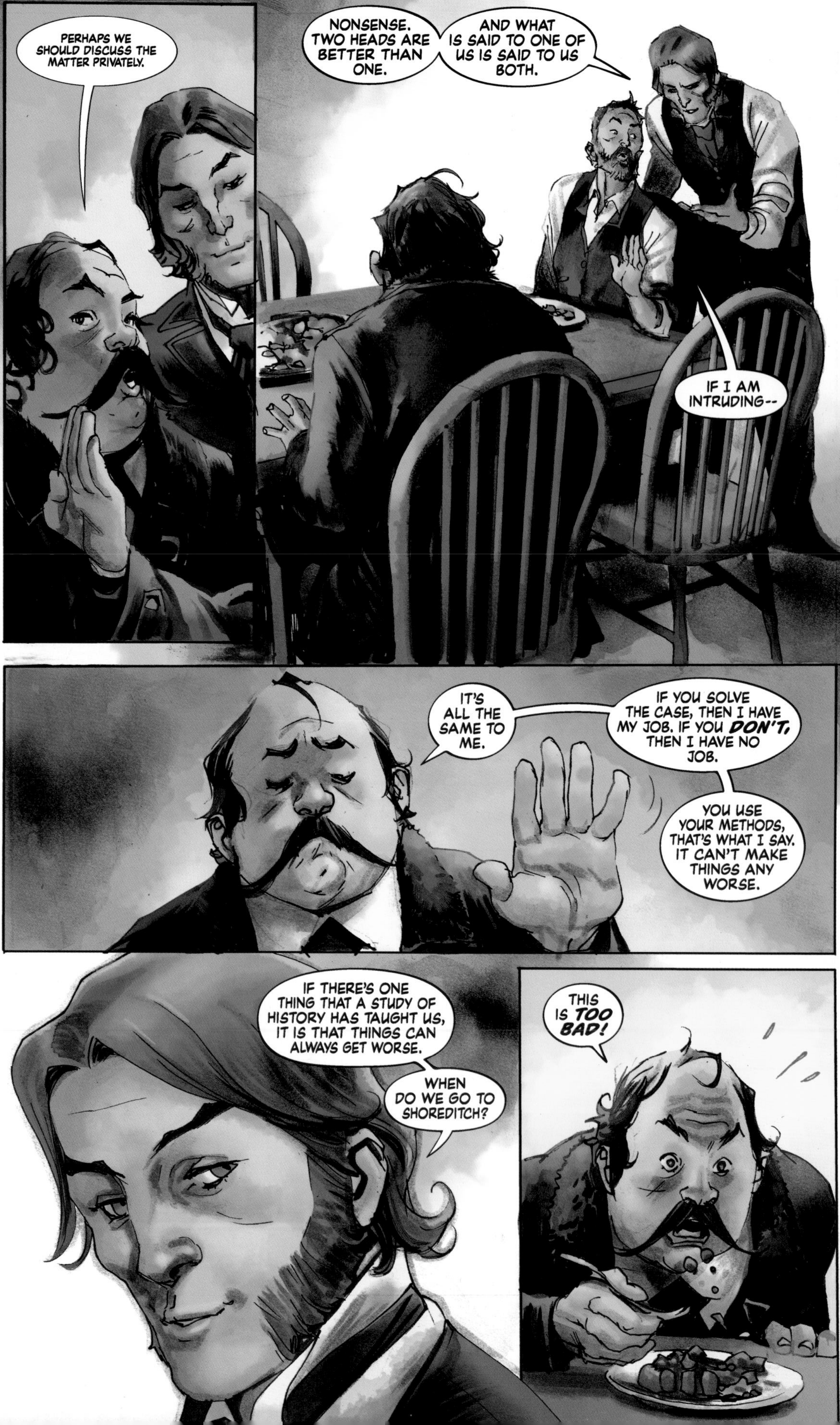
PERHAPS WE SHOULD DISCUSS THE MATTER PRIVATELY.
NONSENSE. TWO HEADS ARE BETTER THAN ONE.
AND WHAT IS SAID TO ONE OF US IS SAID TO US BOTH.
IF I AM INTRUDING--
IT'S ALL THE SAME TO ME.
IF YOU SOLVE THE CASE, THEN I HAVE MY JOB. IF YOU DON'T, THEN I HAVE NO JOB.
YOU USE YOUR METHODS, THAT'S WHAT I SAY. IT CAN'T MAKE THINGS ANY WORSE.
IF THERE'S ONE THING THAT A STUDY OF HISTORY HAS TAUGHT US, IT IS THAT THINGS CAN ALWAYS GET WORSE.
WHEN DO WE GO TO SHOREDITCH?
THIS IS TOO BAD!

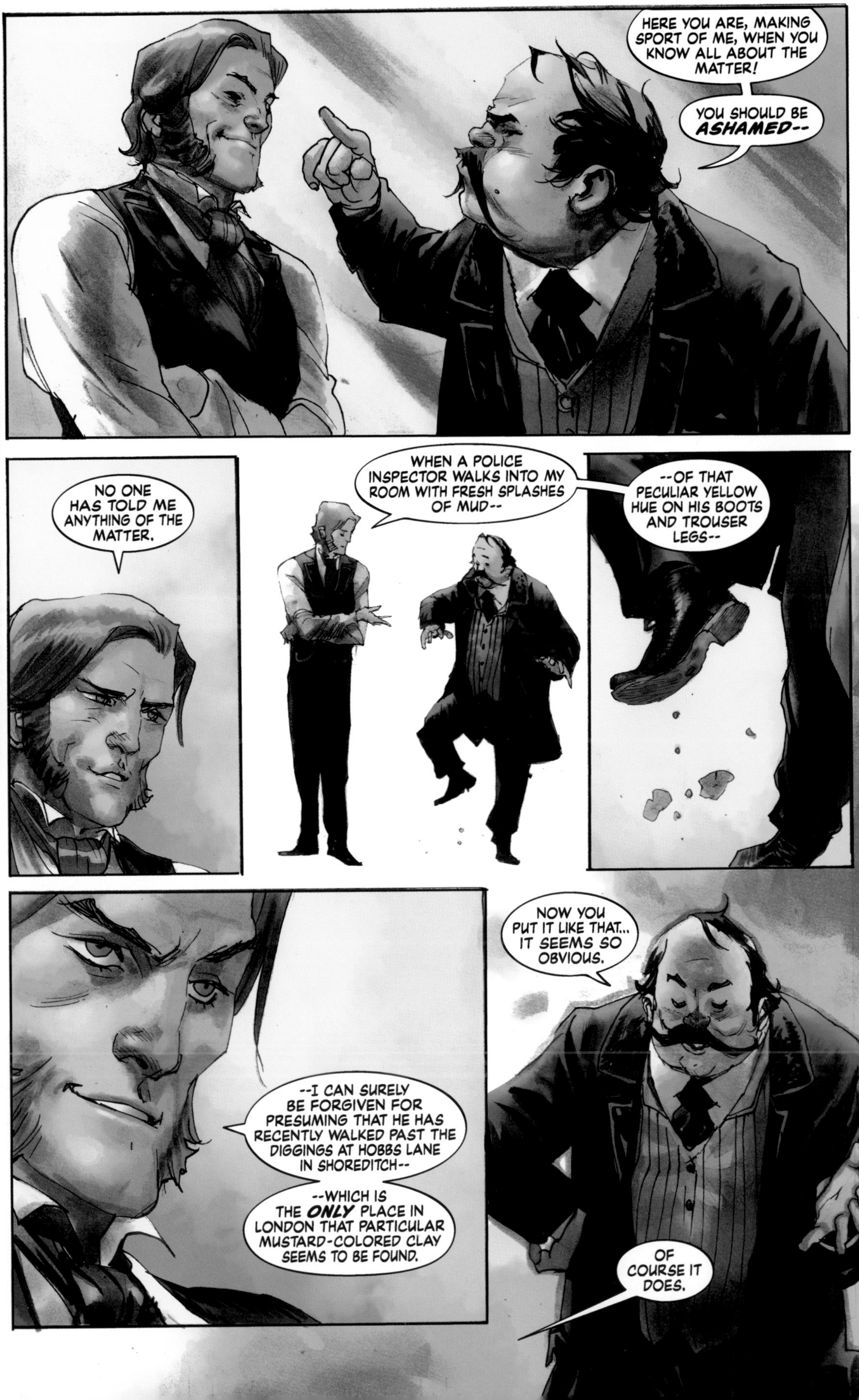
HERE YOU ARE, MAKING SPORT OF ME, WHEN YOU KNOW ALL ABOUT THE MATTER!
YOU SHOULD BE ASHAMED--
NO ONE HAS TOLD ME ANYTHING OF THE MATTER.
WHEN A POLICE INSPECTOR WALKS INTO MY ROOM WITH FRESH SPLASHES OF MUD--
--OF THAT PECULIAR YELLOW HUE ON HIS BOOTS AND TROUSER LEGS--
--I CAN SURELY BE FORGIVEN FOR PRESUMING THAT HE HAS RECENTLY WALKED PAST THE DIGGINGS AT HOBBS LANE IN SHOREDITCH--
--WHICH IS THE ONLY PLACE IN LONDON THAT PARTICULAR MUSTARD-COLORED CLAY SEEMS TO BE FOUND.
NOW YOU PUT IT LIKE THAT... IT SEEMS SO OBVIOUS.
OF COURSE IT DOES.

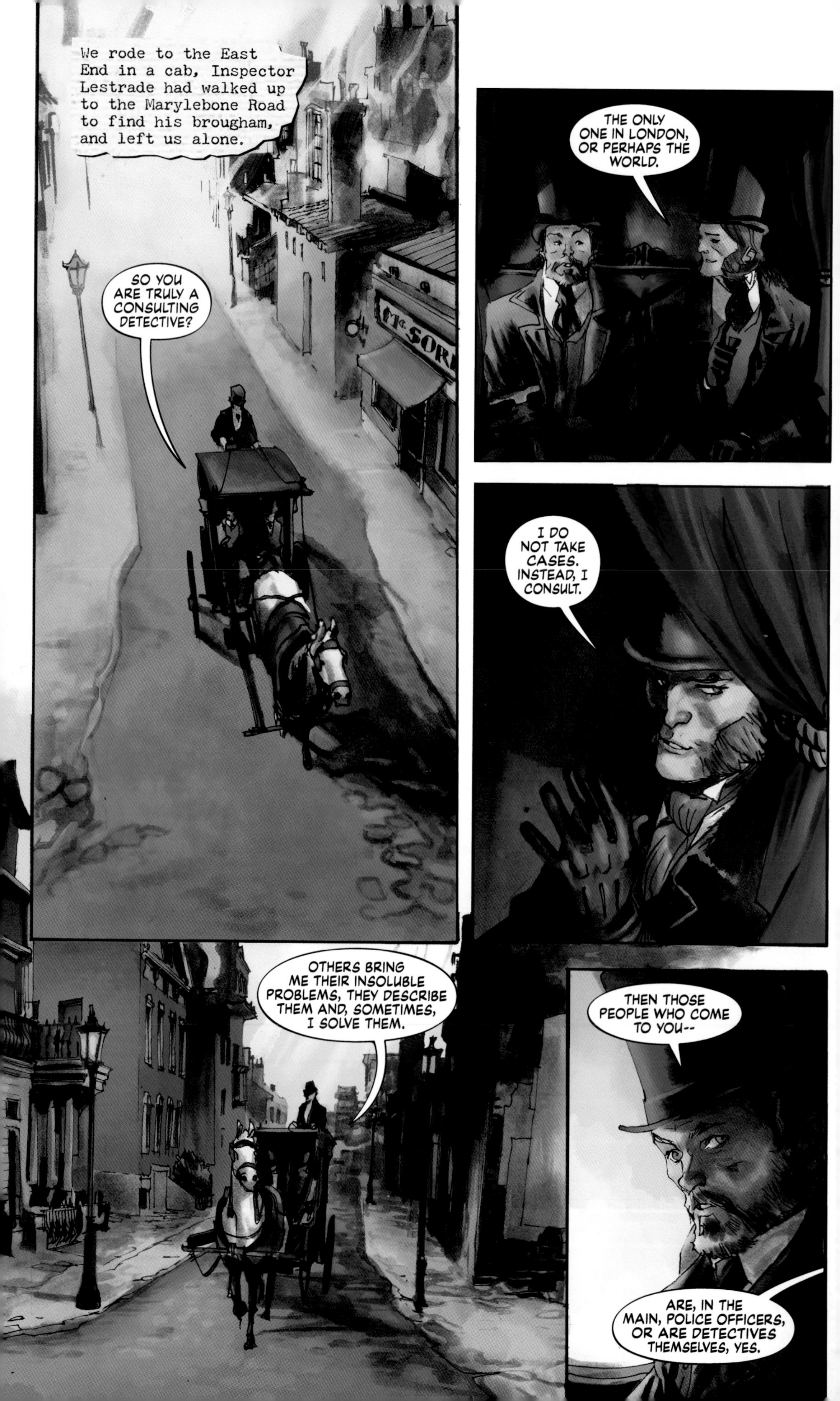
We rode to the East End in a cab, Inspector Lestrade had walked up to the Marylebone Road to find his brougham, and left us alone.
SO YOU ARE TRULY A CONSULTING DETECTIVE?
THE ONLY ONE IN LONDON, OR PERHAPS THE WORLD.
I DO NOT TAKE CASES. INSTEAD, I CONSULT.
OTHERS BRING ME THEIR INSOLUBLE PROBLEMS, THEY DESCRIBE THEM AND, SOMETIMES, I SOLVE THEM.
THEN THOSE PEOPLE WHO COME TO YOU--
ARE, IN THE MAIN, POLICE OFFICERS, OR ARE DETECTIVES THEMSELVES, YES.

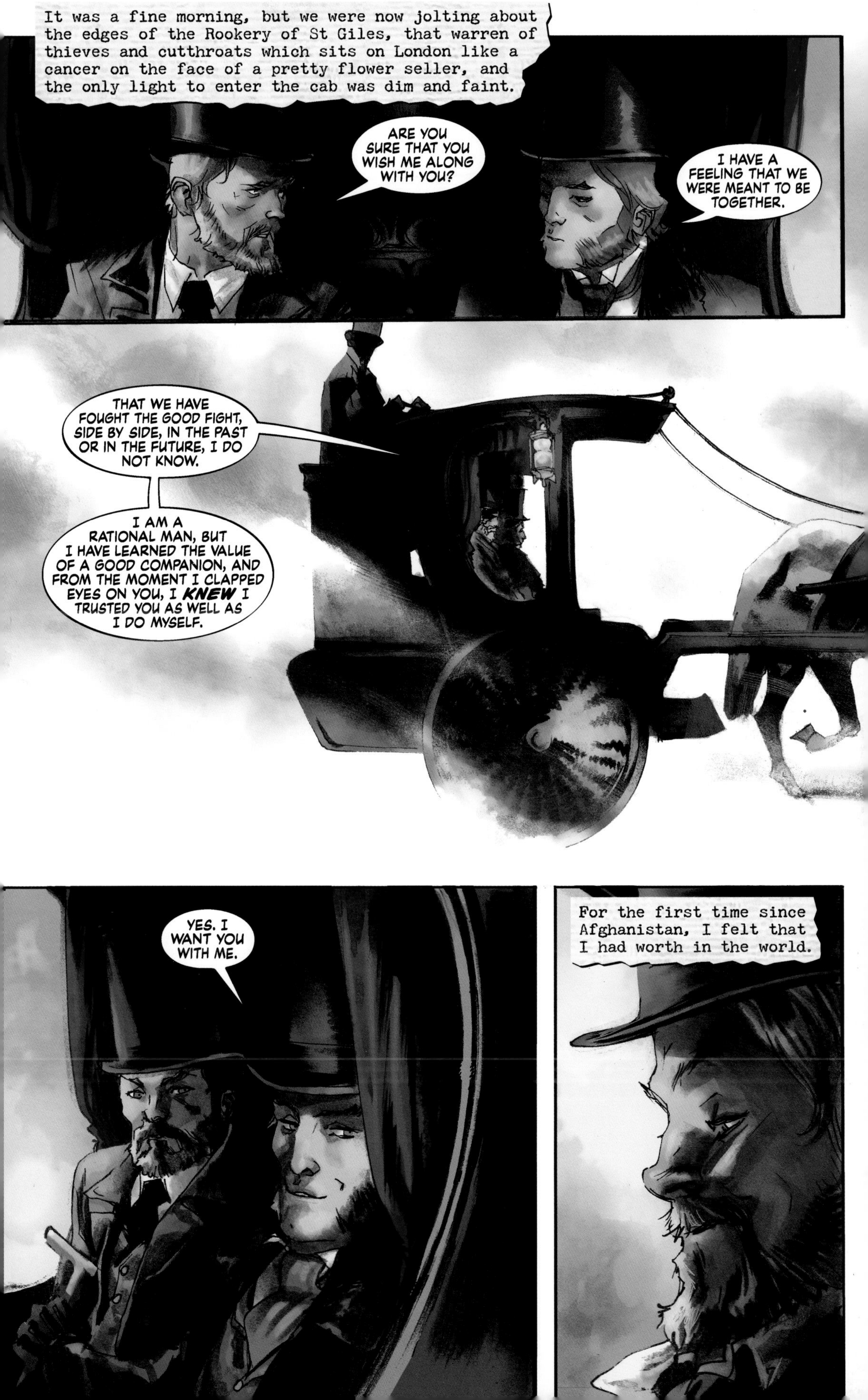

It was a fine morning, but we were now jolting about the edges of the Rookery of St Giles, that warren of thieves and cutthroats which sits on London like a cancer on the face of a pretty flower seller, and the only light to enter the cab was dim and faint.
ARE YOU SURE THAT YOU WISH ME ALONG WITH YOU?
I HAVE A FEELING THAT WE WERE MEANT TO BE TOGETHER.
THAT WE HAVE FOUGHT THE GOOD FIGHT, SIDE BY SIDE, IN THE PAST OR IN THE FUTURE, I DO NOT KNOW.
I AM A RATIONAL MAN, BUT I HAVE LEARNED THE VALUE OF A GOOD COMPANION, AND FROM THE MOMENT I CLAPPED EYES ON YOU, I ***KNEW*** I TRUSTED YOU AS WELL AS I DO MYSELF.
YES. I WANT YOU WITH ME.
For the first time since Afghanistan, I felt that I had worth in the world.

THE ROOM

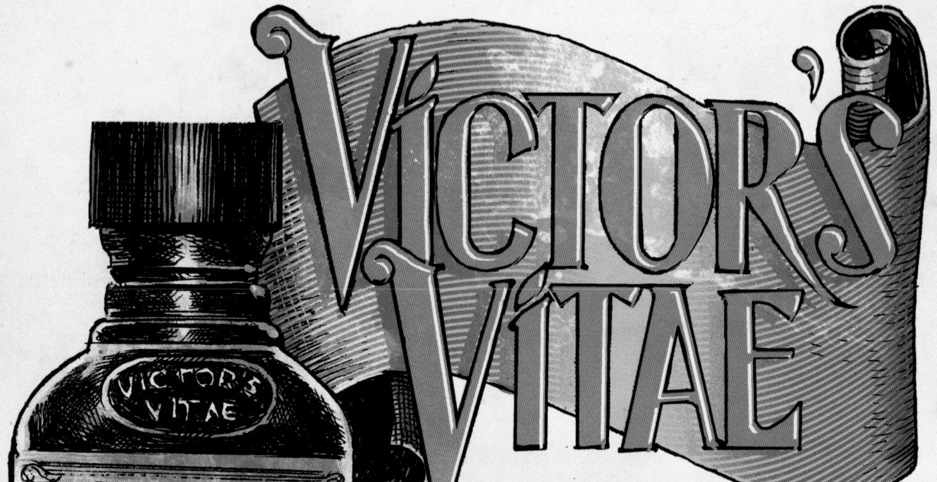
VICTOR'S VITAE
VICTOR'S VITAE
VITAE
Victor's *"Vitae"!*
An electrical fluid! Do your limbs and nether regions lack of life? Do you look back on the days of your youth with envy? Are the pleasures of the flesh now buried and forgot? **Victor's *"Vitae"*** will bring life where life has long been lost: even the oldest warhorse can be a proud stallion once more! Bringing Life to the Dead: from an old family recipe and the best of modern science. To receive signed attestations of the efficacy of **Victor's *"Vitae"*** write to the V. von F. Company, 1b Cheap Street, London.

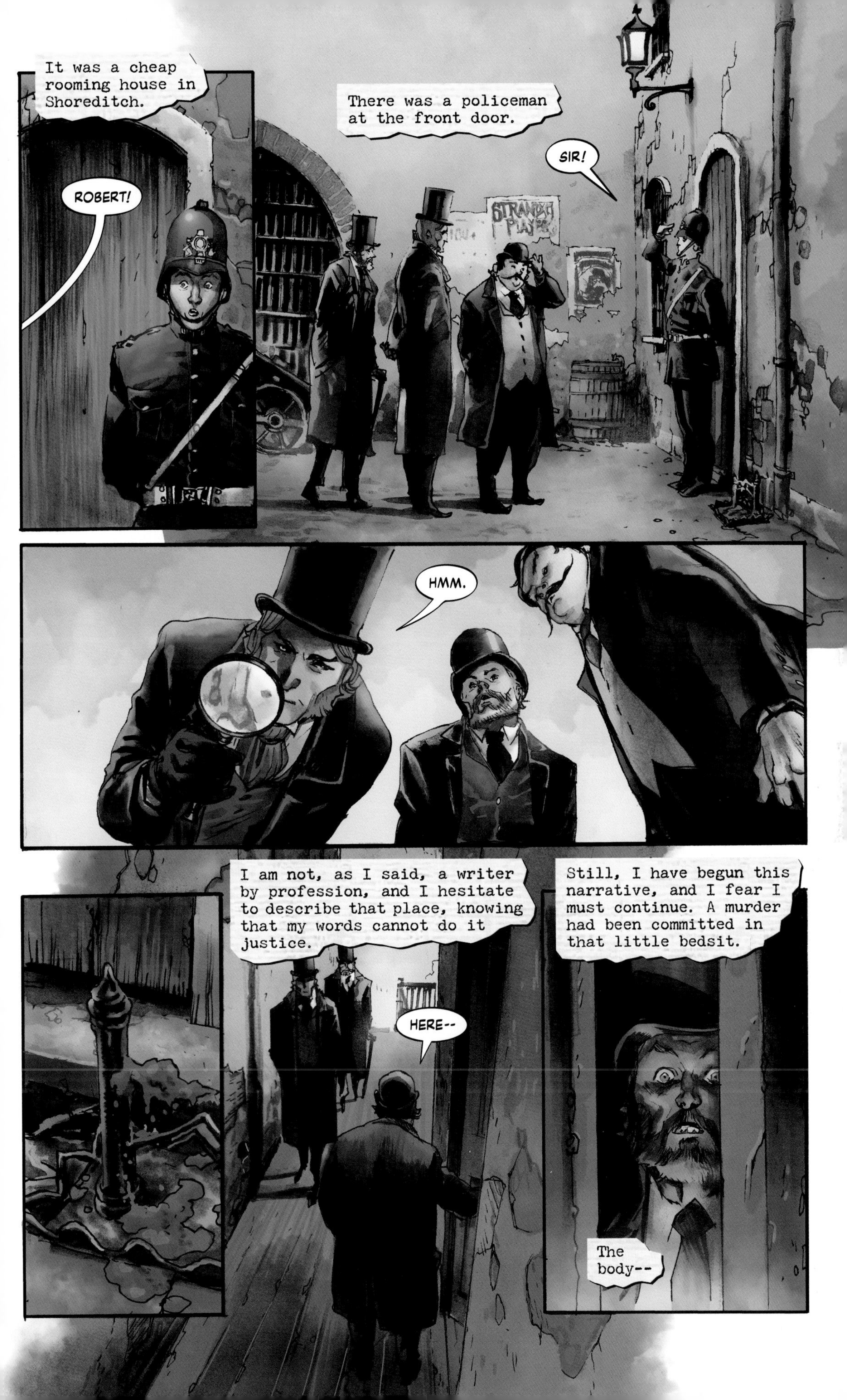
It was a cheap rooming house in Shoreditch.
ROBERT!
There was a policeman at the front door.
SIR!
HMM.
I am not, as I said, a writer by profession, and I hesitate to describe that place, knowing that my words cannot do it justice.
HERE--
Still, I have begun this narrative, and I fear I must continue. A murder had been committed in that little bedsit.
The body--

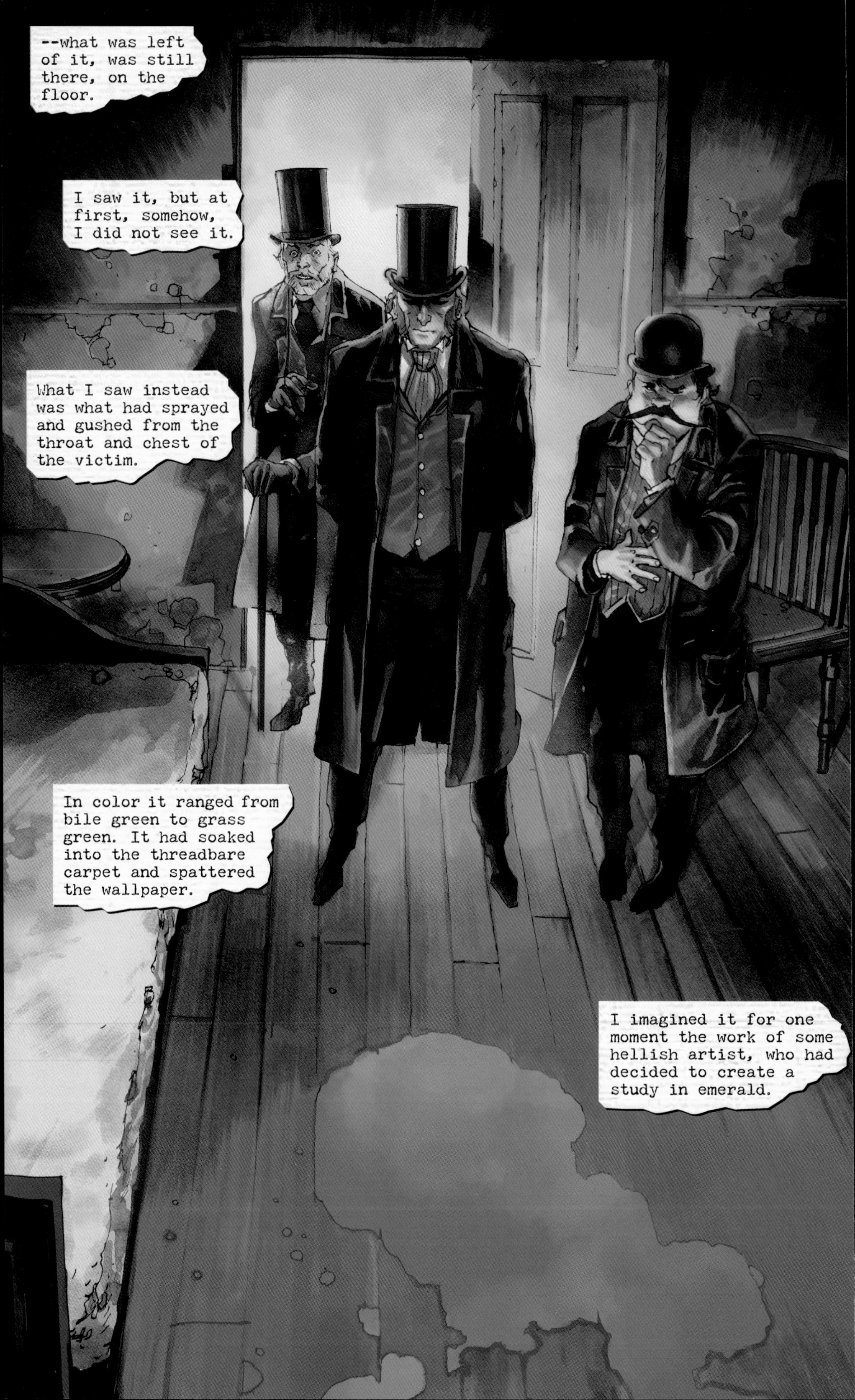
--what was left of it, was still there, on the floor.
I saw it, but at first, somehow, I did not see it.
What I saw instead was what had sprayed and gushed from the throat and chest of the victim.
In color it ranged from bile green to grass green. It had soaked into the threadbare carpet and spattered the wallpaper.
I imagined it for one moment the work of some hellish artist, who had decided to create a study in emerald.

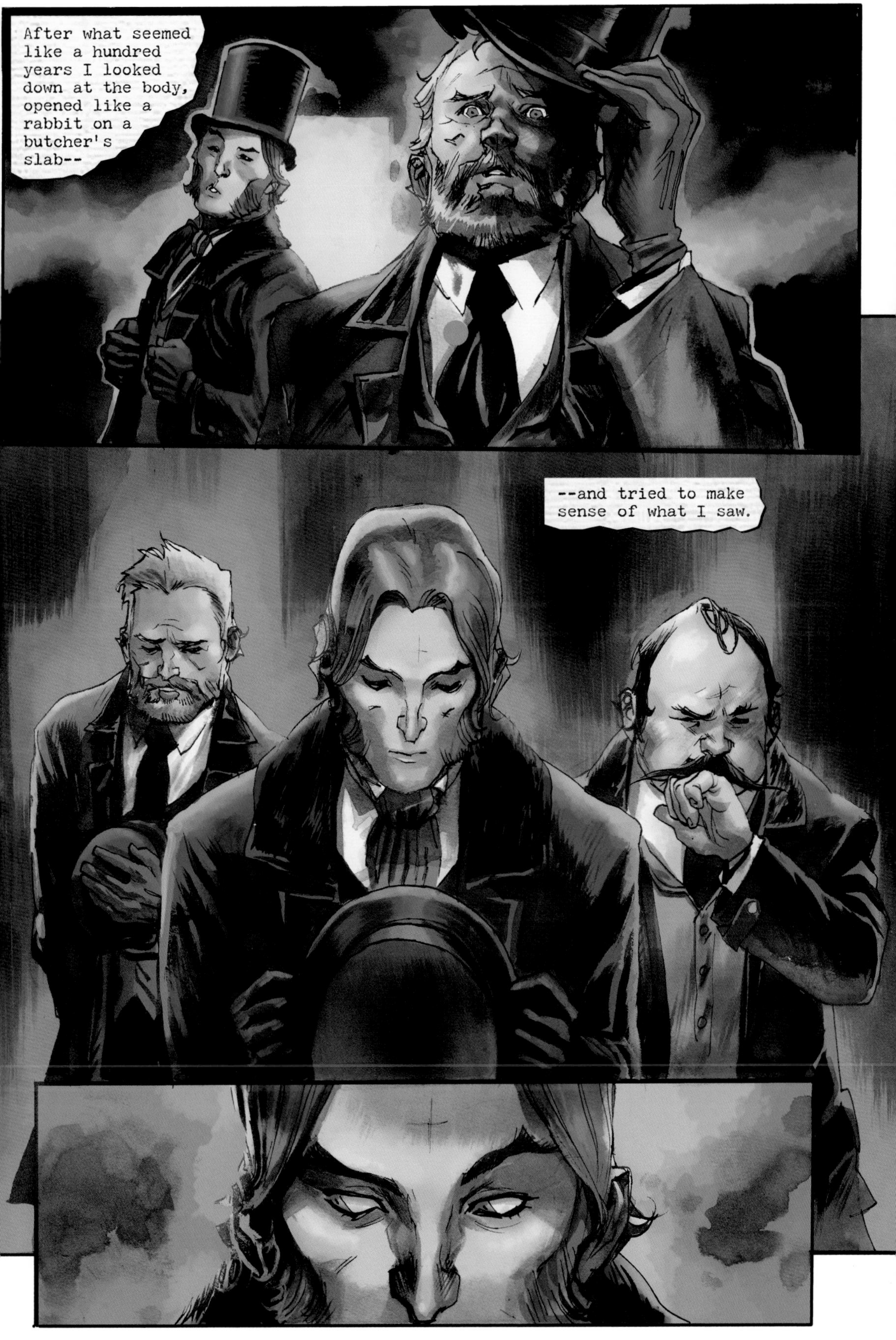
After what seemed like a hundred years I looked down at the body, opened like a rabbit on a butcher's slab--
--and tried to make sense of what I saw.

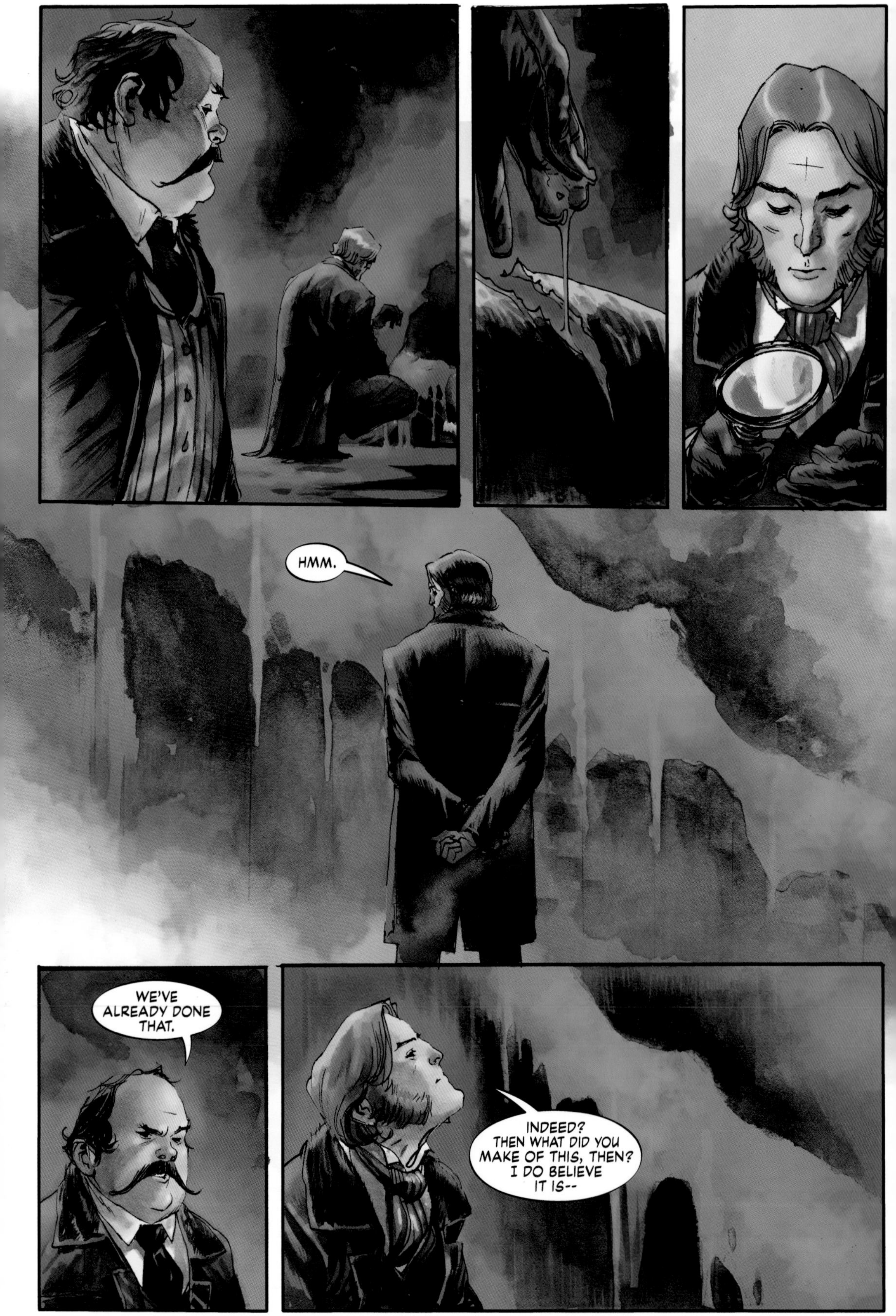
HMM.
WE'VE ALREADY DONE THAT.
INDEED? THEN WHAT DID YOU MAKE OF THIS, THEN? I DO BELIEVE IT IS--

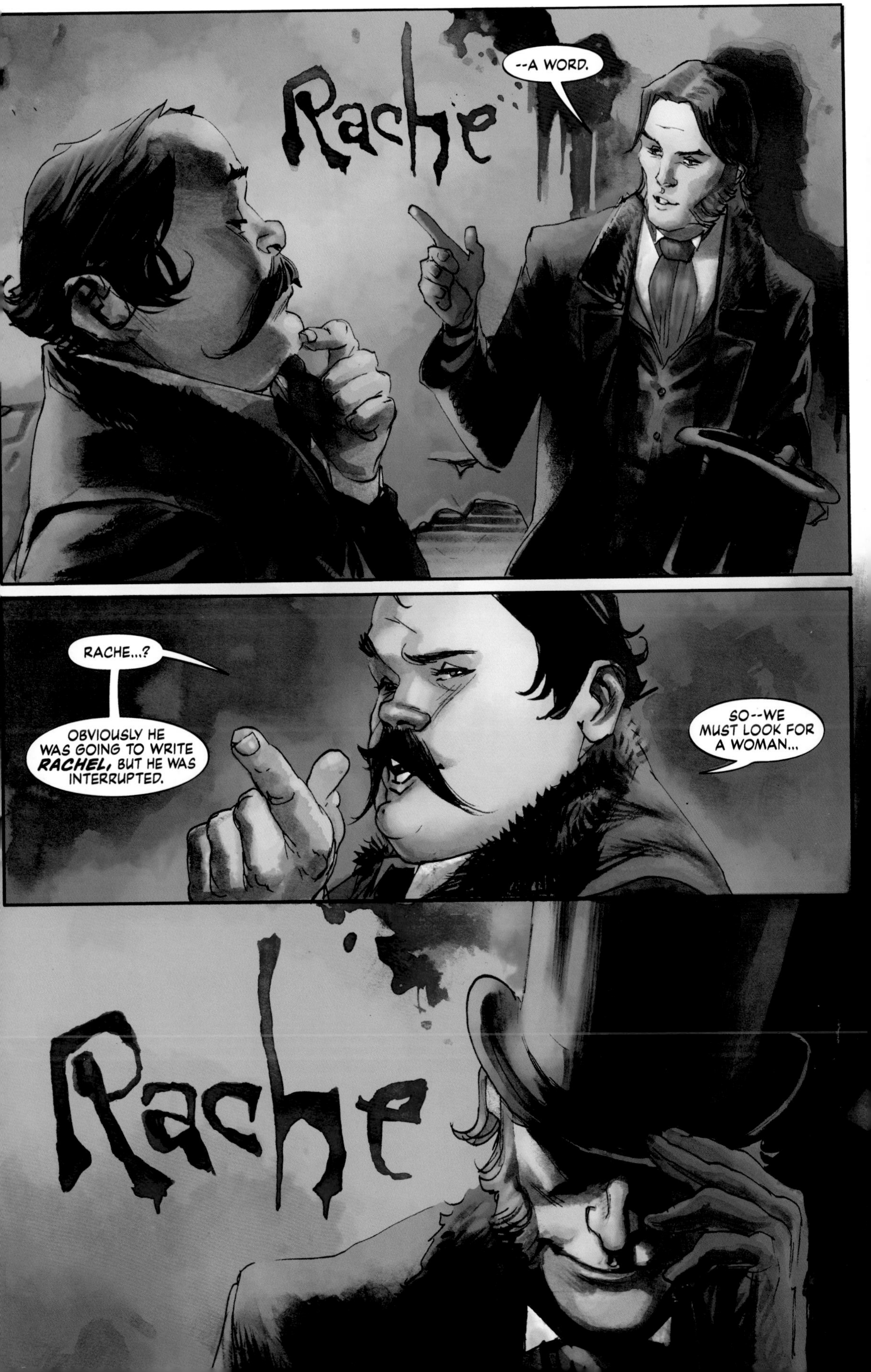

Rache
--A WORD.
RACHE...?
OBVIOUSLY HE WAS GOING TO WRITE ***RACHEL,*** BUT HE WAS INTERRUPTED.
SO--WE MUST LOOK FOR A WOMAN...
Rache

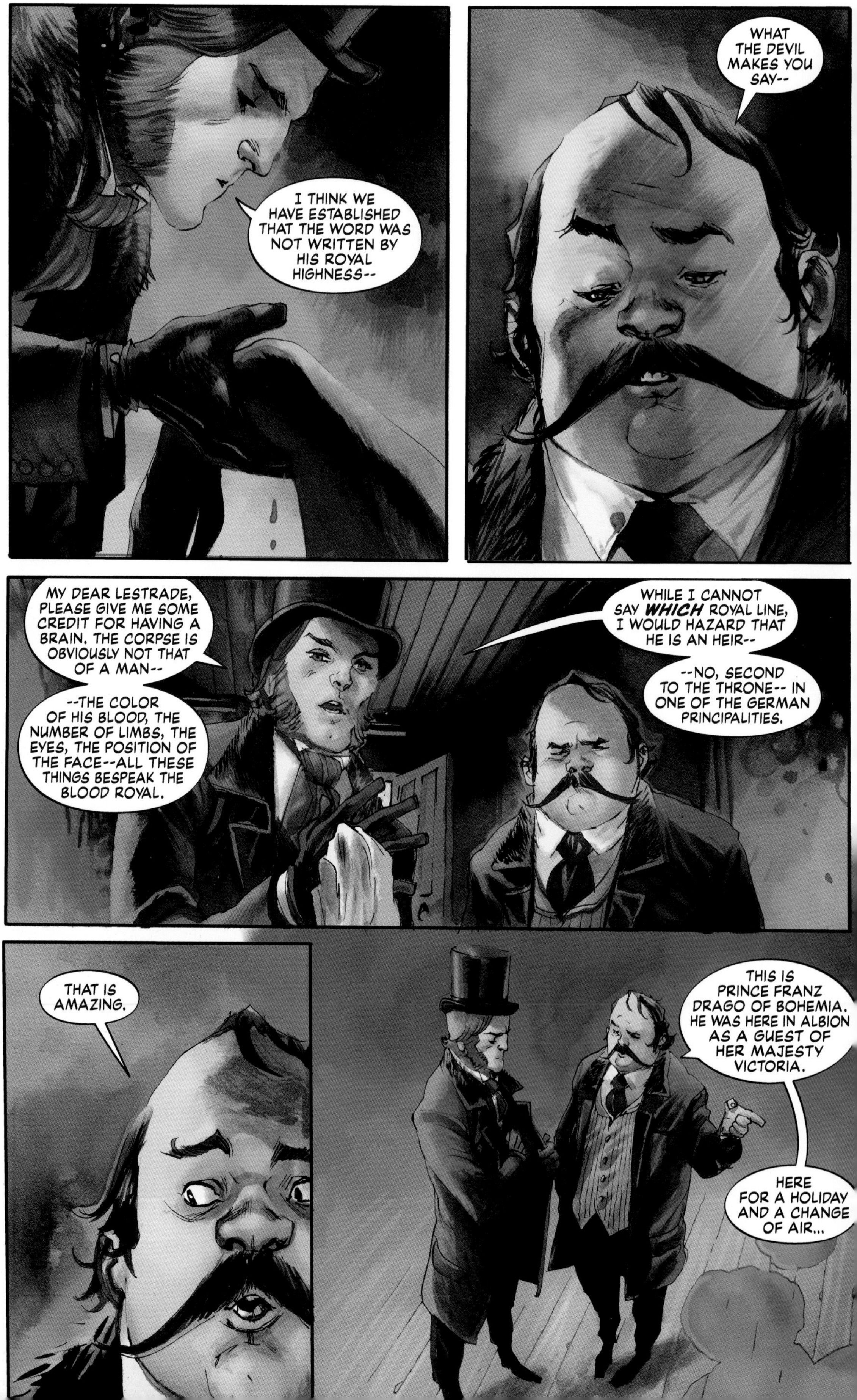
I THINK WE HAVE ESTABLISHED THAT THE WORD WAS NOT WRITTEN BY HIS ROYAL HIGHNESS--
WHAT THE DEVIL MAKES YOU SAY--
MY DEAR LESTRADE, PLEASE GIVE ME SOME CREDIT FOR HAVING A BRAIN. THE CORPSE IS OBVIOUSLY NOT THAT OF A MAN--
--THE COLOR OF HIS BLOOD, THE NUMBER OF LIMBS, THE EYES, THE POSITION OF THE FACE--ALL THESE THINGS BESPEAK THE BLOOD ROYAL.
WHILE I CANNOT SAY **WHICH** ROYAL LINE, I WOULD HAZARD THAT HE IS AN HEIR--
--NO, SECOND TO THE THRONE-- IN ONE OF THE GERMAN PRINCIPALITIES.
THAT IS AMAZING.
THIS IS PRINCE FRANZ DRAGO OF BOHEMIA. HE WAS HERE IN ALBION AS A GUEST OF HER MAJESTY VICTORIA.
HERE FOR A HOLIDAY AND A CHANGE OF AIR...

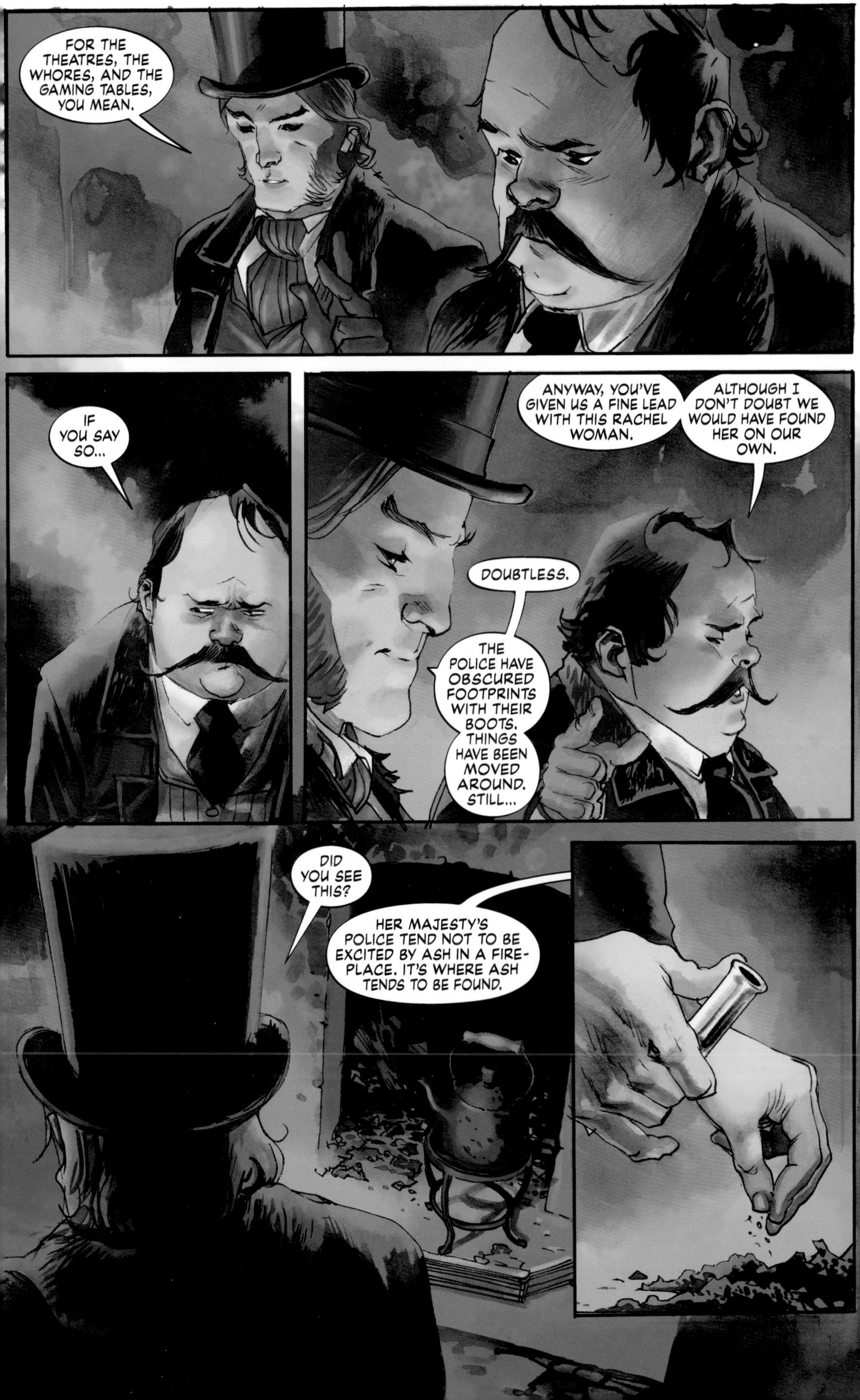
FOR THE THEATRES, THE WHORES, AND THE GAMING TABLES, YOU MEAN.
IF YOU SAY SO...
ANYWAY, YOU'VE GIVEN US A FINE LEAD WITH THIS RACHEL WOMAN.
ALTHOUGH I DON'T DOUBT WE WOULD HAVE FOUND HER ON OUR OWN.
DOUBTLESS.
THE POLICE HAVE OBSCURED FOOTPRINTS WITH THEIR BOOTS. THINGS HAVE BEEN MOVED AROUND. STILL...
DID YOU SEE THIS?
HER MAJESTY'S POLICE TEND NOT TO BE EXCITED BY ASH IN A FIRE-PLACE. IT'S WHERE ASH TENDS TO BE FOUND.

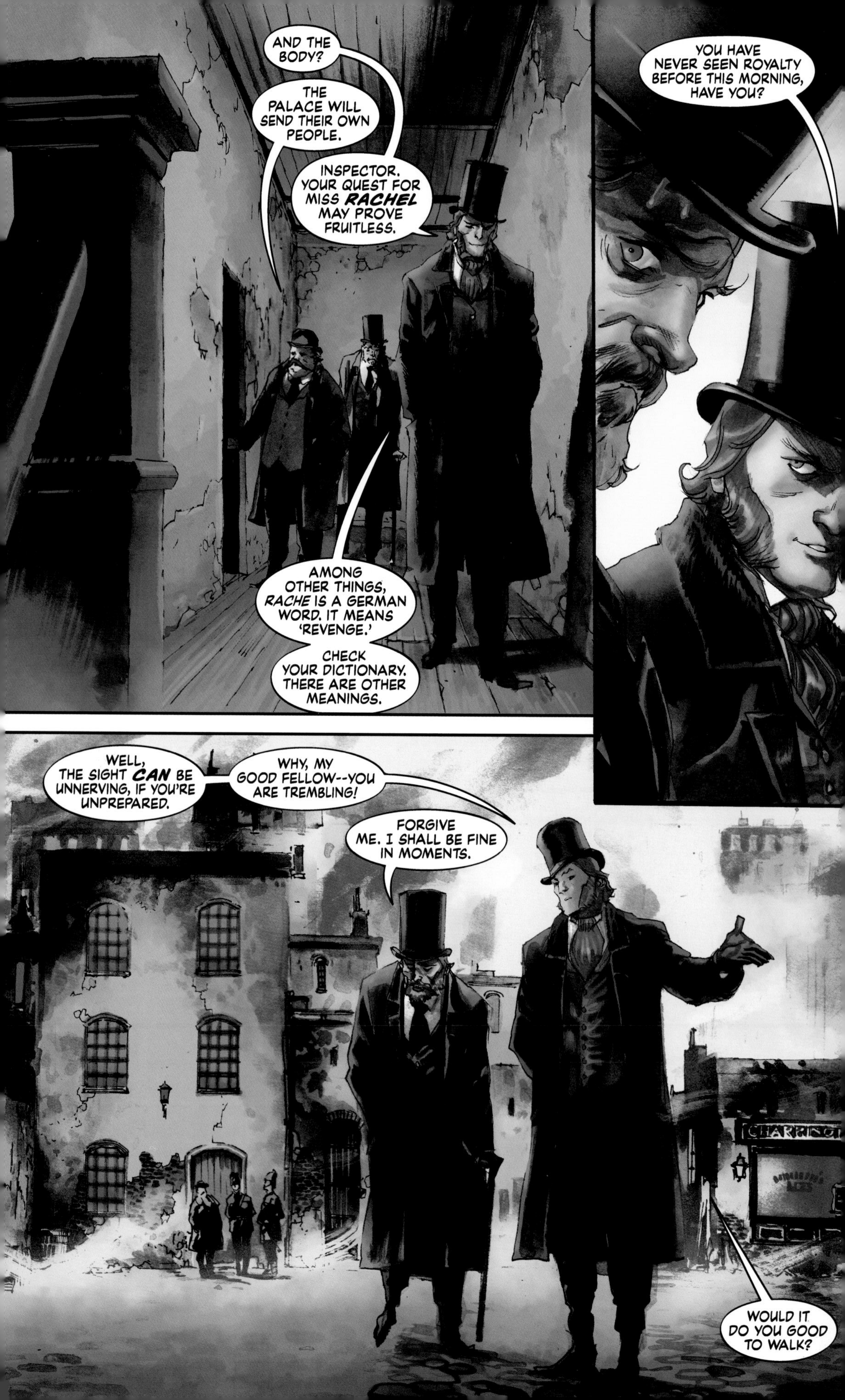
AND THE BODY?
THE PALACE WILL SEND THEIR OWN PEOPLE.
INSPECTOR. YOUR QUEST FOR MISS *RACHEL* MAY PROVE FRUITLESS.
AMONG OTHER THINGS, *RACHE* IS A GERMAN WORD. IT MEANS 'REVENGE.'
CHECK YOUR DICTIONARY. THERE ARE OTHER MEANINGS.
YOU HAVE NEVER SEEN ROYALTY BEFORE THIS MORNING, HAVE YOU?
WELL, THE SIGHT **CAN** BE UNNERVING, IF YOU'RE UNPREPARED.
WHY, MY GOOD FELLOW--YOU ARE TREMBLING!
FORGIVE ME. I SHALL BE FINE IN MOMENTS.
WOULD IT DO YOU GOOD TO WALK?

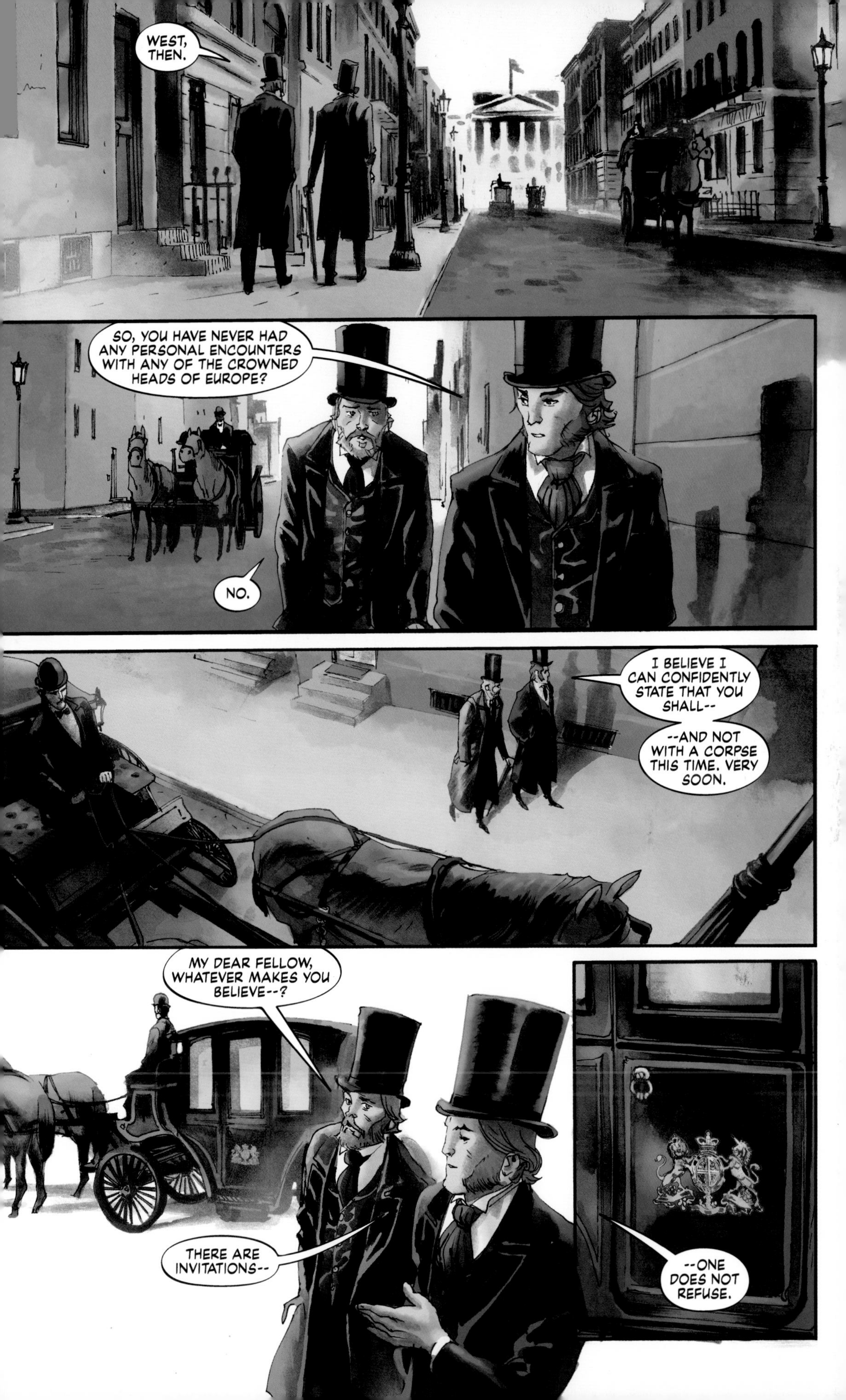
WEST, THEN.
SO, YOU HAVE NEVER HAD ANY PERSONAL ENCOUNTERS WITH ANY OF THE CROWNED HEADS OF EUROPE?
NO.
I BELIEVE I CAN CONFIDENTLY STATE THAT YOU SHALL--
--AND NOT WITH A CORPSE THIS TIME. VERY SOON.
MY DEAR FELLOW, WHATEVER MAKES YOU BELIEVE--?
THERE ARE INVITATIONS--
--ONE DOES NOT REFUSE.

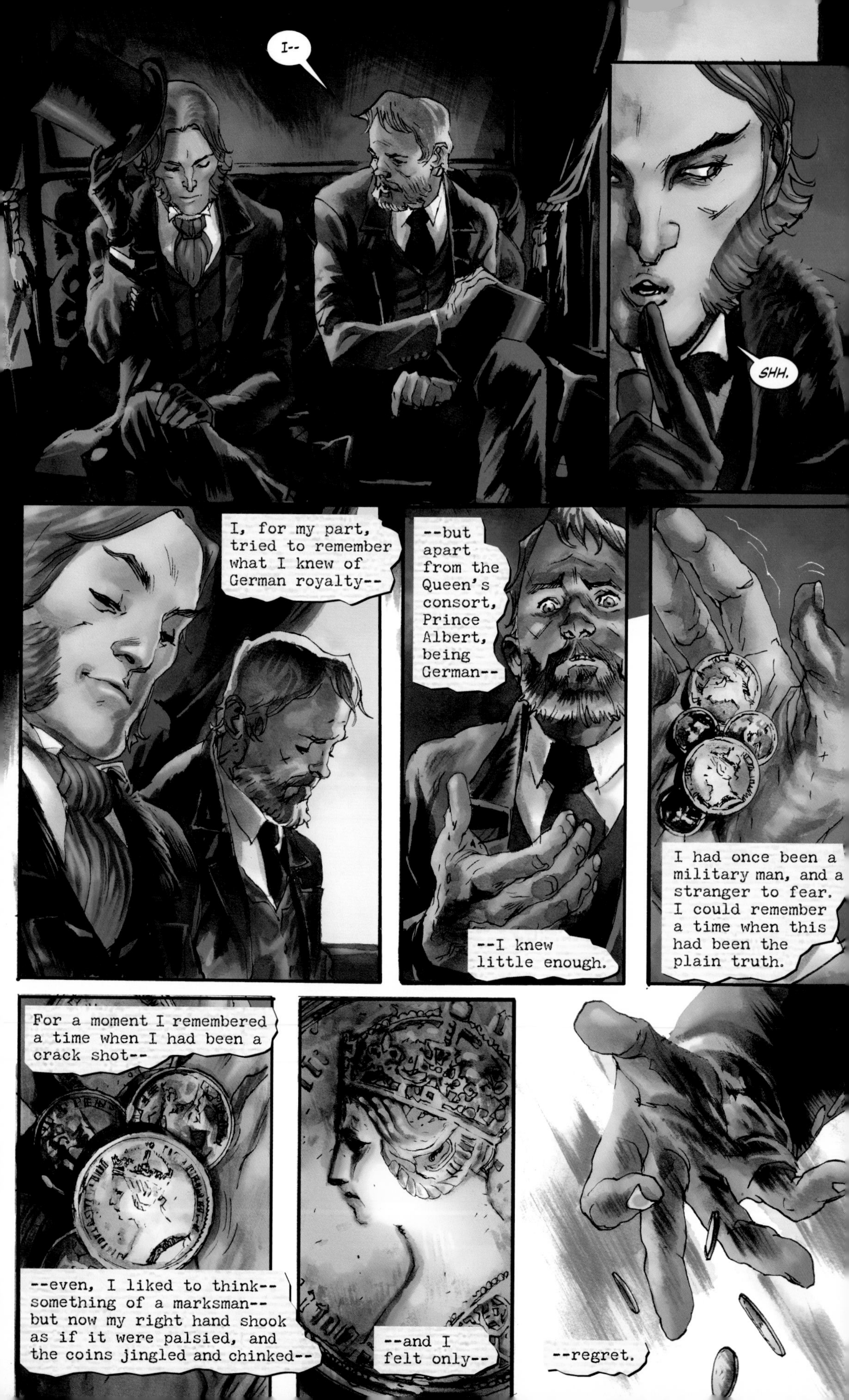
I--
SHH.
I, for my part, tried to remember what I knew of German royalty--
--but apart from the Queen's consort, Prince Albert, being German--
--I knew little enough.
I had once been a military man, and a stranger to fear. I could remember a time when this had been the plain truth.
For a moment I remembered a time when I had been a crack shot--
--even, I liked to think--something of a marksman--but now my right hand shook as if it were palsied, and the coins jingled and chinked--
--and I felt only--
--regret.

THE PALACE

before

At Long Last Doctor Henry Jekyll is proud to announce the general release of the world-renowned **"Jekyll's Powders"** for popular consumption. No longer the province of the privileged few. **Release the Inner You!** For Inner and Outer Cleanliness! **TOO MANY PEOPLE,** both men and women, suffer from **CONSTIPATION OF THE SOUL!**

Relief is immediate and cheap – with Jekyll's powders!
(Available in Vanilla and Original Mentholatum Formulations.)

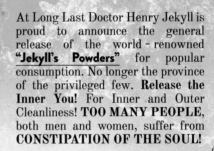

JEKYLL'S
POWDERS

after

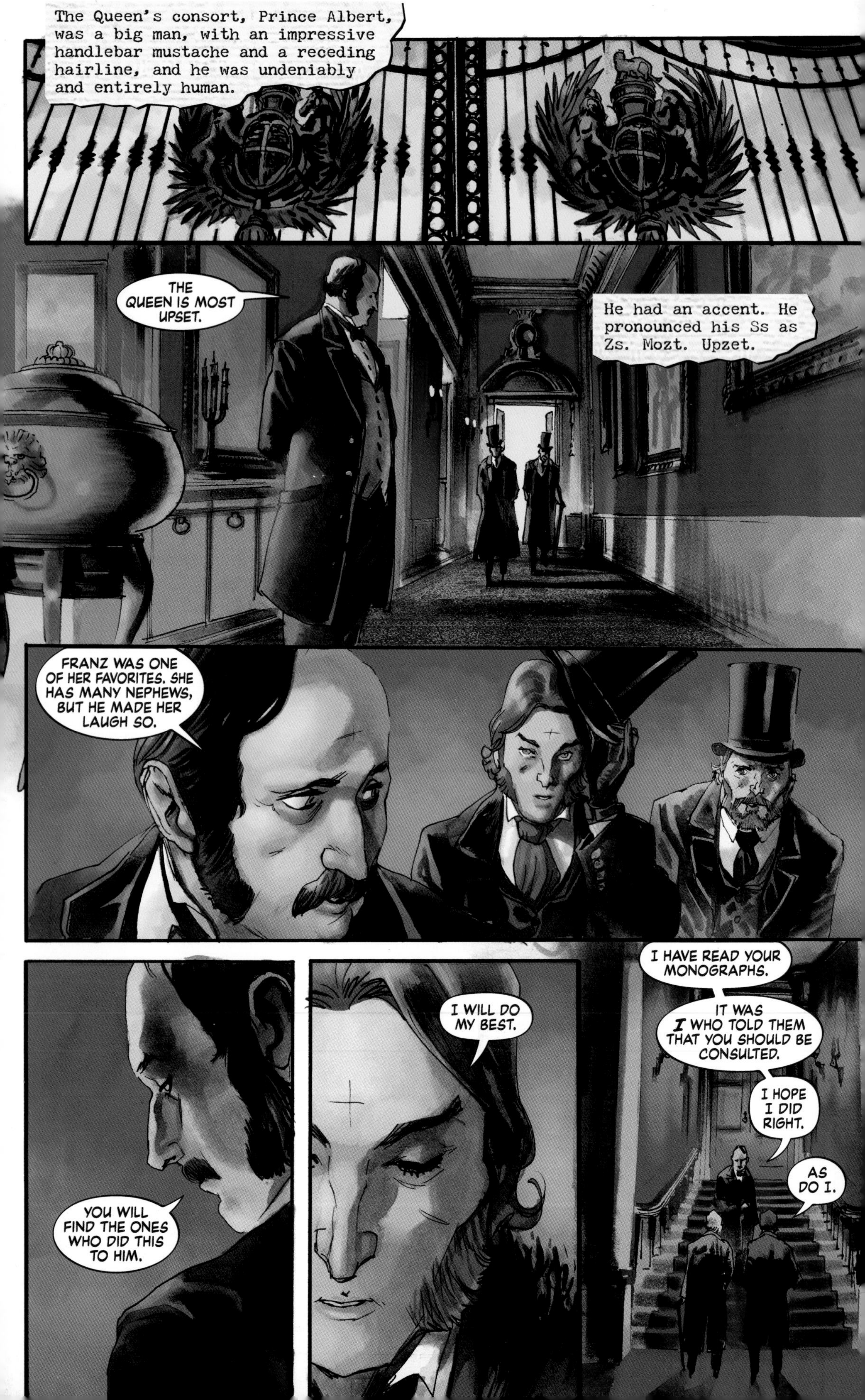
The Queen's consort, Prince Albert, was a big man, with an impressive handlebar mustache and a receding hairline, and he was undeniably and entirely human.
THE QUEEN IS MOST UPSET.
He had an accent. He pronounced his Ss as Zs. Mozt. Upzet.
FRANZ WAS ONE OF HER FAVORITES. SHE HAS MANY NEPHEWS, BUT HE MADE HER LAUGH SO.
YOU WILL FIND THE ONES WHO DID THIS TO HIM.
I WILL DO MY BEST.
I HAVE READ YOUR MONOGRAPHS.
IT WAS *I* WHO TOLD THEM THAT YOU SHOULD BE CONSULTED.
I HOPE I DID RIGHT.
AS DO I.

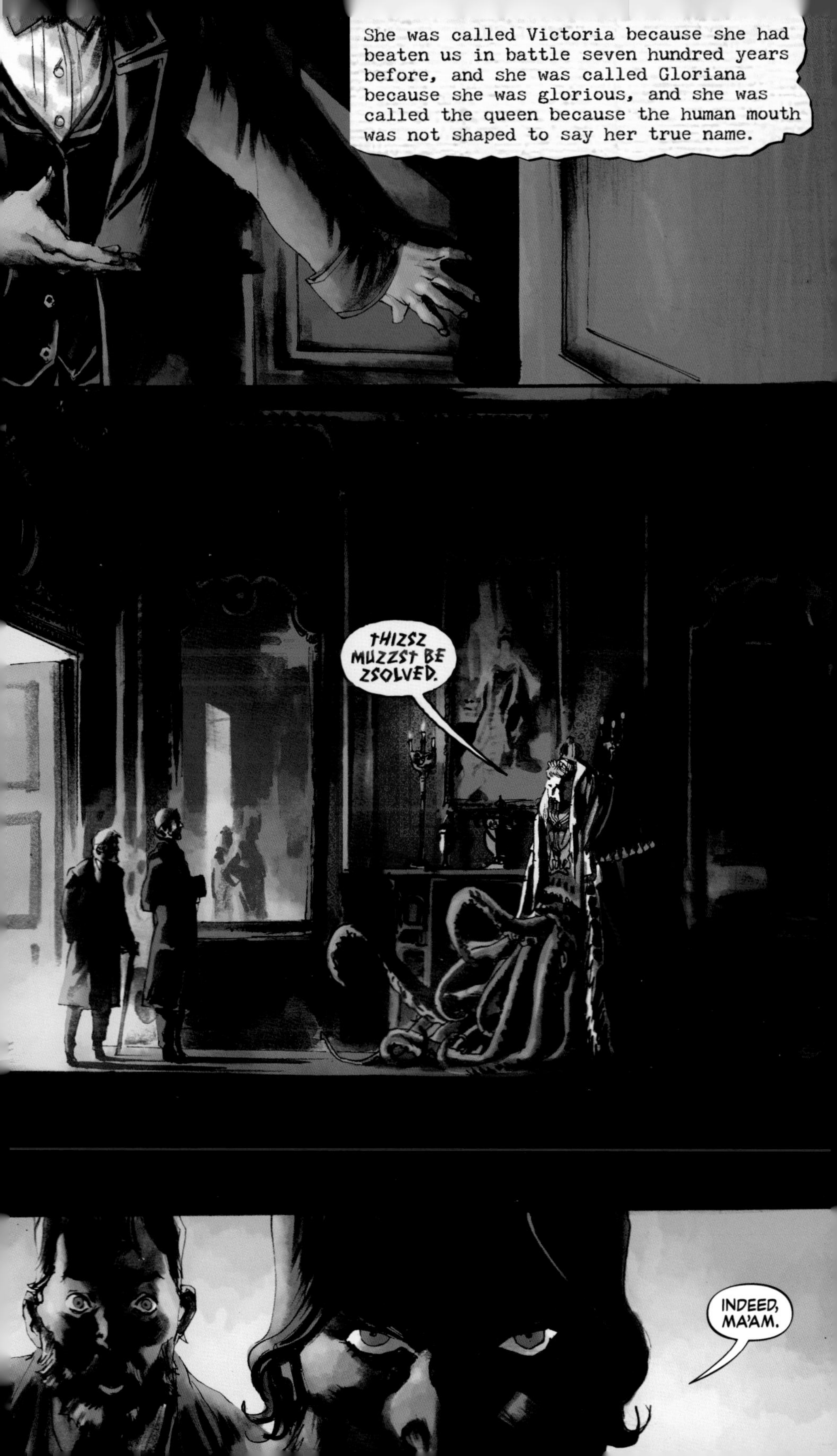

She was called Victoria because she had beaten us in battle seven hundred years before, and she was called Gloriana because she was glorious, and she was called the queen because the human mouth was not shaped to say her true name.
THIZSZ MUZZST BE ZSOLVED.
INDEED, MA'AM.

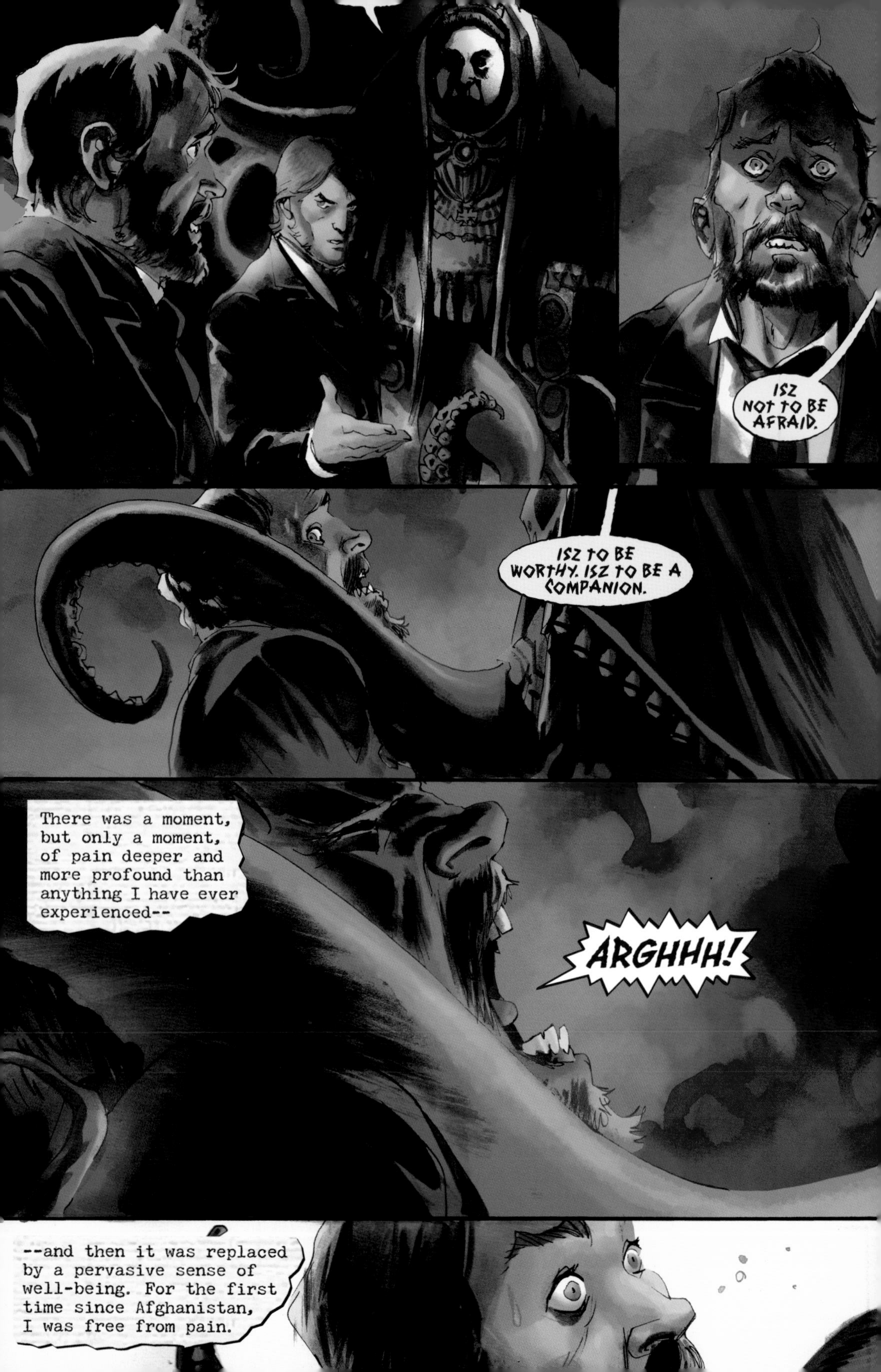
ISZ NOT TO BE AFRAID.
ISZ TO BE WORTHY. ISZ TO BE A COMPANION.
There was a moment, but only a moment, of pain deeper and more profound than anything I have ever experienced--
ARGHHH!
--and then it was replaced by a pervasive sense of well-being. For the first time since Afghanistan, I was free from pain.

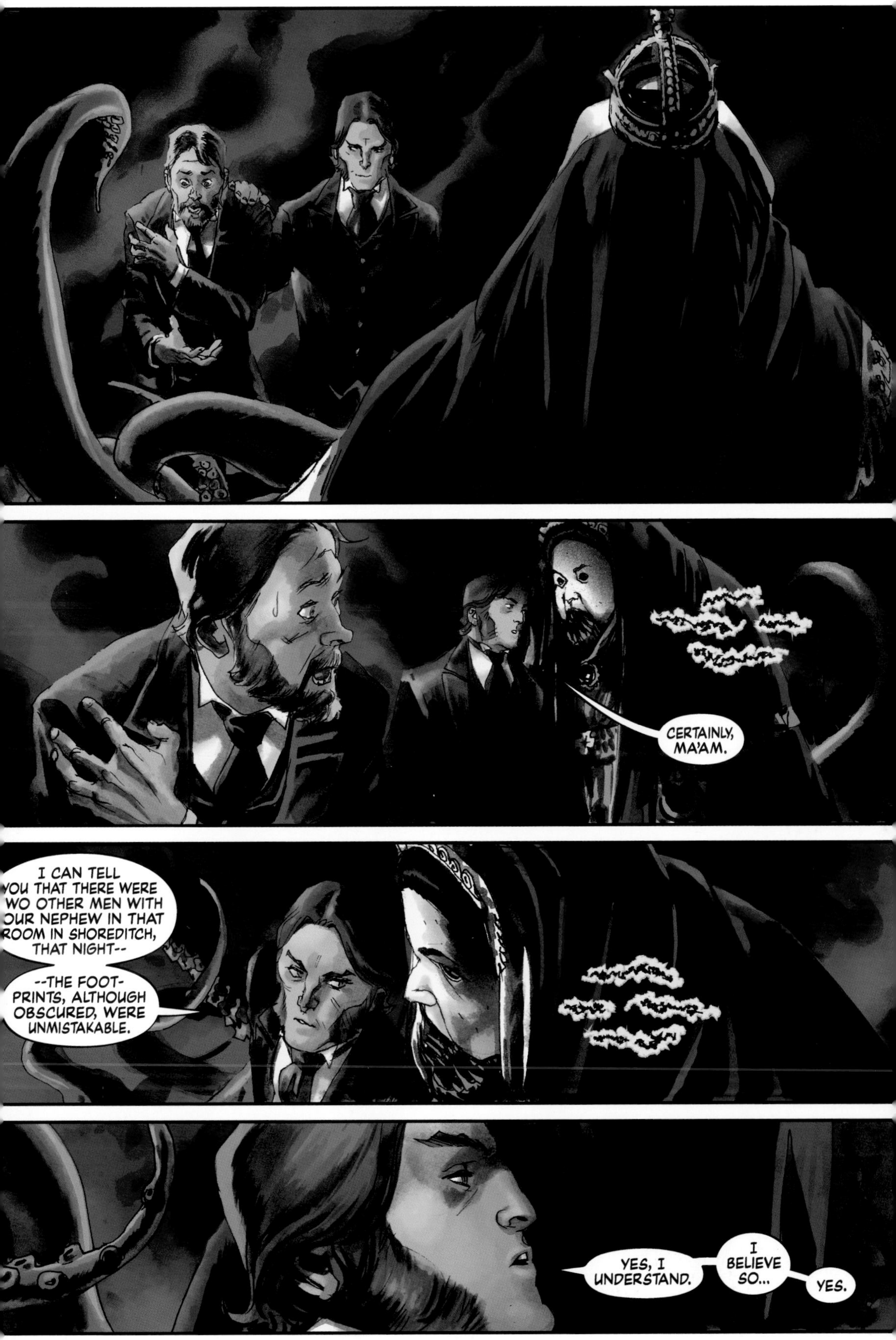
CERTAINLY, MA'AM.
I CAN TELL YOU THAT THERE WERE TWO OTHER MEN WITH OUR NEPHEW IN THAT ROOM IN SHOREDITCH, THAT NIGHT--
--THE FOOT-PRINTS, ALTHOUGH OBSCURED, WERE UNMISTAKABLE.
YES, I UNDERSTAND.
I BELIEVE SO...
YES.

He was quiet when we left and said nothing to me as we rode back to Baker Street.

It was dark already.

I wondered how long we had spent in the Palace.

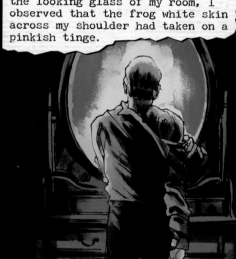

Upon our return to Baker Street, in the looking glass of my room, I observed that the frog white skin across my shoulder had taken on a pinkish tinge.

I hoped that I was not imagining it--

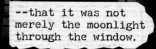

--that it was not merely the moonlight through the window.

THE PERFORMANCE

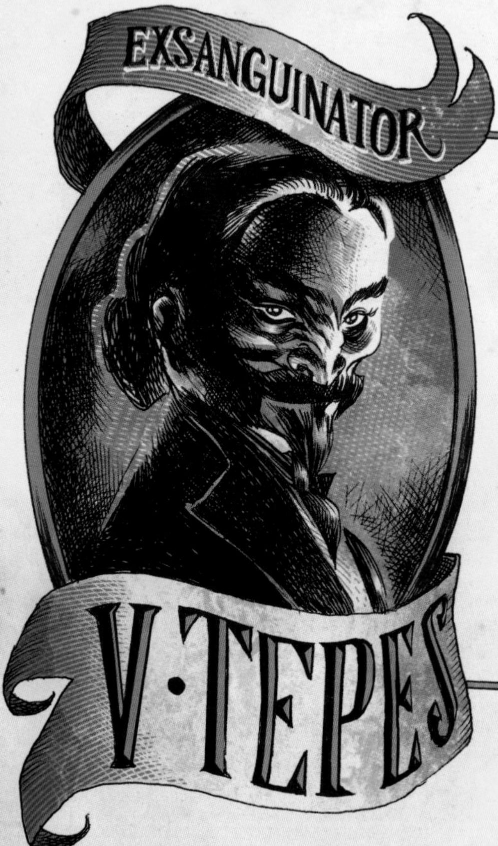
EXSANGUINATOR
V·TEPES

LIVER COMPLAINTS?!
BILIOUS ATTACKS?!
NEURASTHENIC DISTURBANCES?!
QUINSY?!
ARTHRITIS?!

These are just a handful of the *complaints* for which a professional **EXSANGUINATION** can be the *remedy*. In our offices we have sheaves of **TESTIMONIALS** which can be inspected by the public at *any time*. Do not put your health in the hands of *amateurs*!! We have been doing this for a very long time:
V. TEPES - PROFESSIONAL EXSANGUINATOR. (Remember! It is pronounced *Tzsep-pesh*!) Romania, Paris, London, Whitby. **You've tried the rest - NOW TRY THE BEST!!**

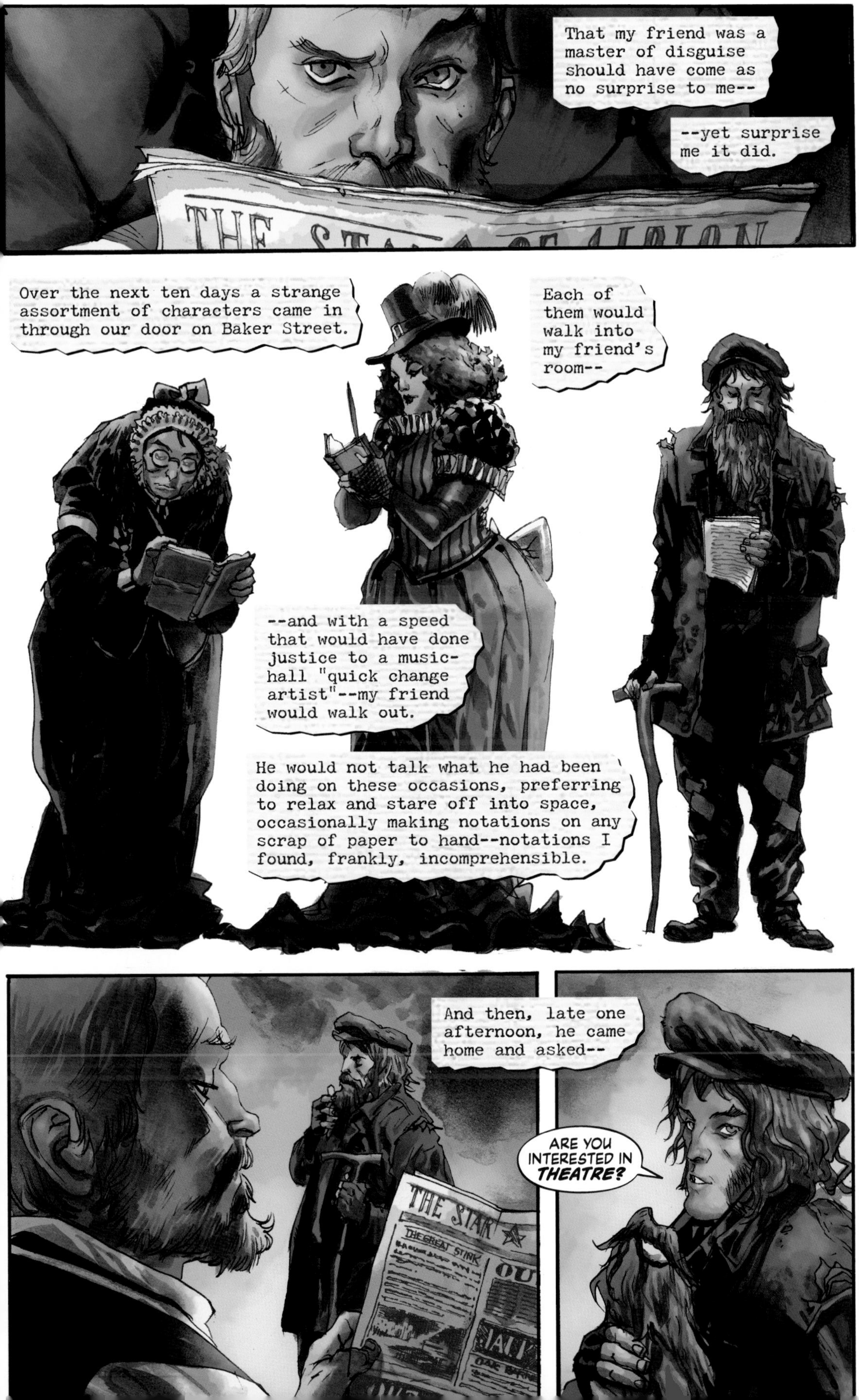
That my friend was a master of disguise should have come as no surprise to me--
--yet surprise me it did.
Over the next ten days a strange assortment of characters came in through our door on Baker Street.
Each of them would walk into my friend's room--
--and with a speed that would have done justice to a music-hall "quick change artist"--my friend would walk out.
He would not talk what he had been doing on these occasions, preferring to relax and stare off into space, occasionally making notations on any scrap of paper to hand--notations I found, frankly, incomprehensible.
And then, late one afternoon, he came home and asked--
THE STAR
THE GREAT STINK
ARE YOU INTERESTED IN THEATRE?

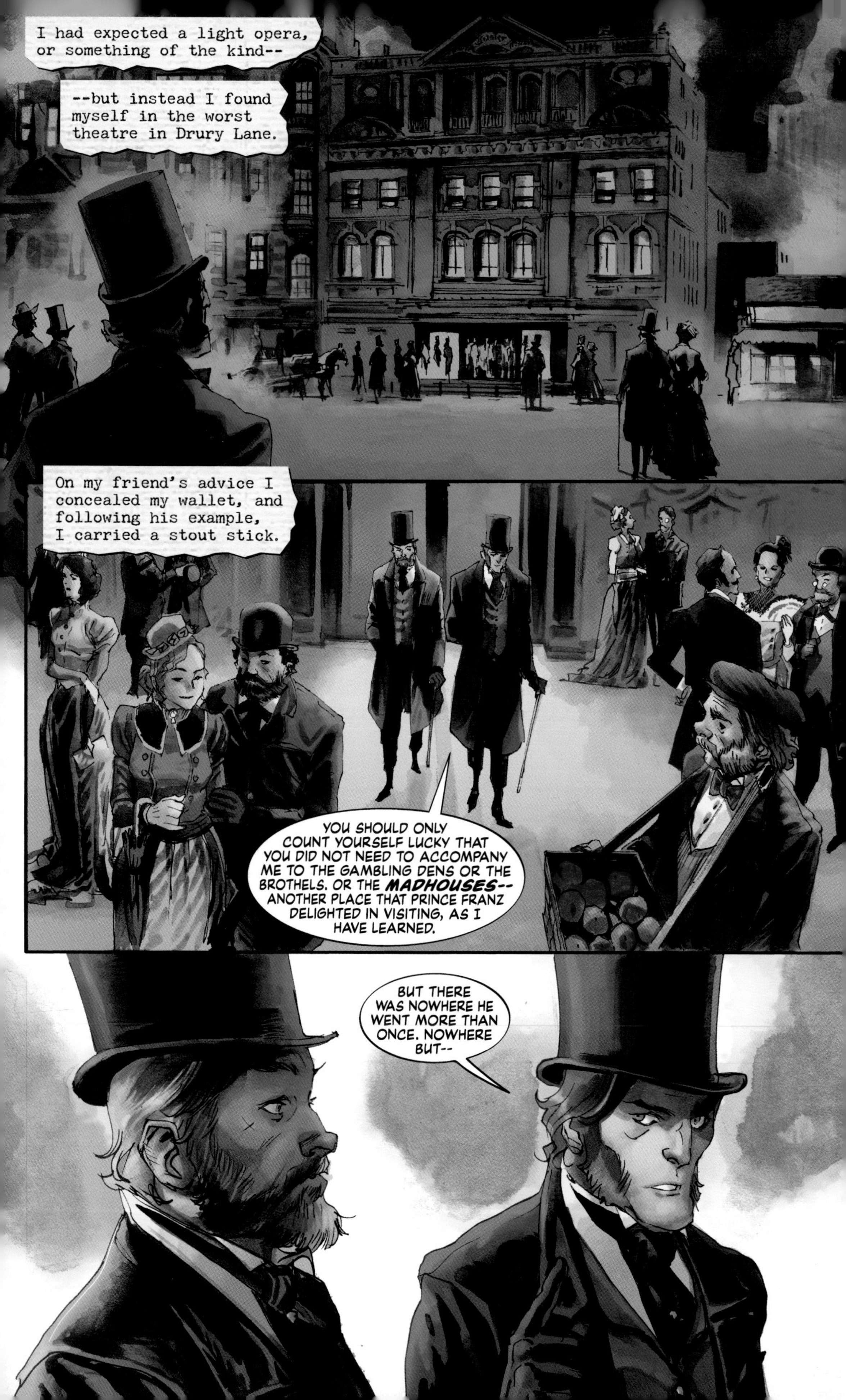
I had expected a light opera, or something of the kind--
--but instead I found myself in the worst theatre in Drury Lane.
On my friend's advice I concealed my wallet, and following his example, I carried a stout stick.
YOU SHOULD ONLY COUNT YOURSELF LUCKY THAT YOU DID NOT NEED TO ACCOMPANY ME TO THE GAMBLING DENS OR THE BROTHELS. OR THE MADHOUSES-- ANOTHER PLACE THAT PRINCE FRANZ DELIGHTED IN VISITING, AS I HAVE LEARNED.
BUT THERE WAS NOWHERE HE WENT MORE THAN ONCE. NOWHERE BUT--

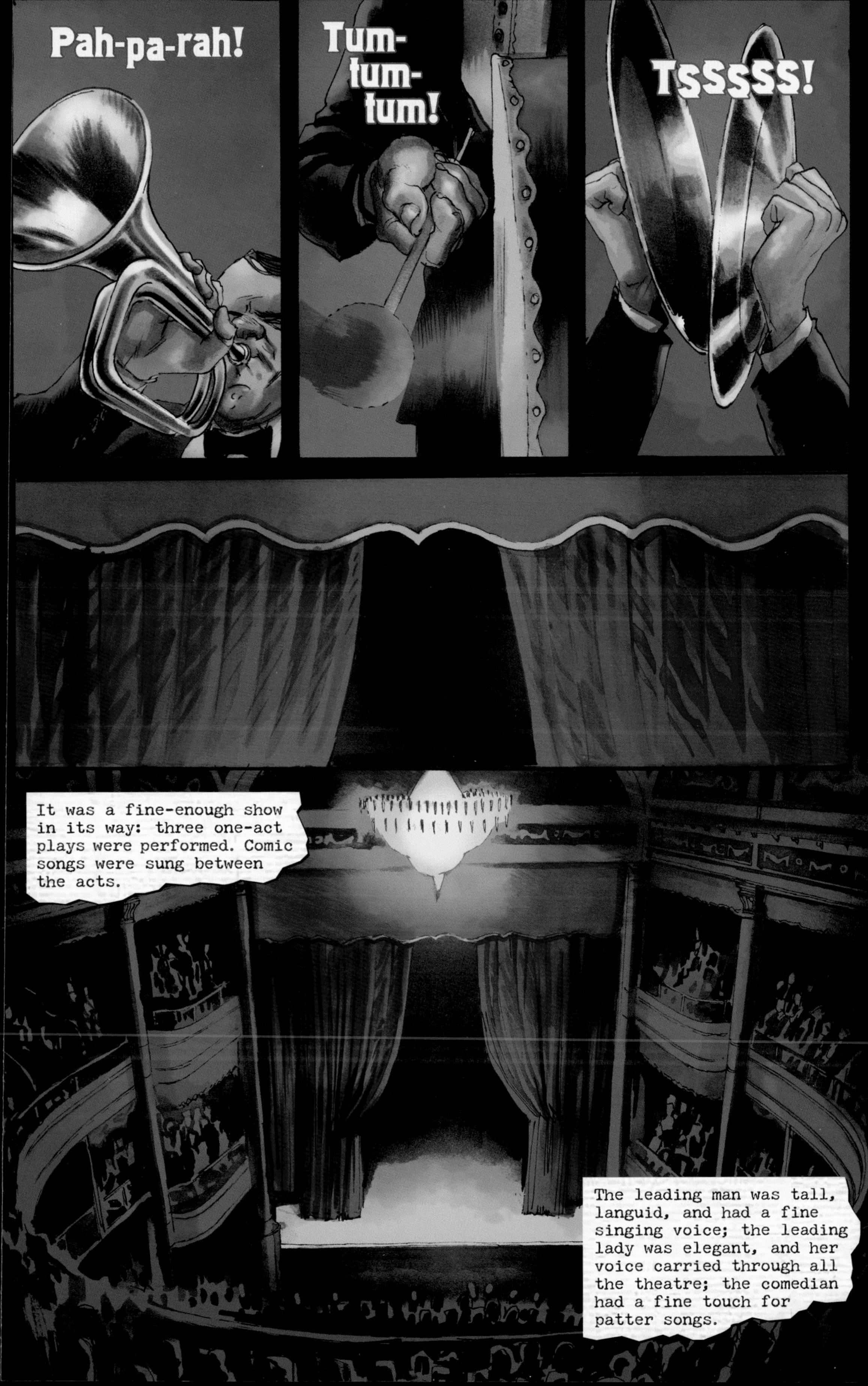

Pah-pa-rah!
Tum-tum-tum!
Tsssss!
It was a fine-enough show in its way: three one-act plays were performed. Comic songs were sung between the acts.
The leading man was tall, languid, and had a fine singing voice; the leading lady was elegant, and her voice carried through all the theatre; the comedian had a fine touch for patter songs.

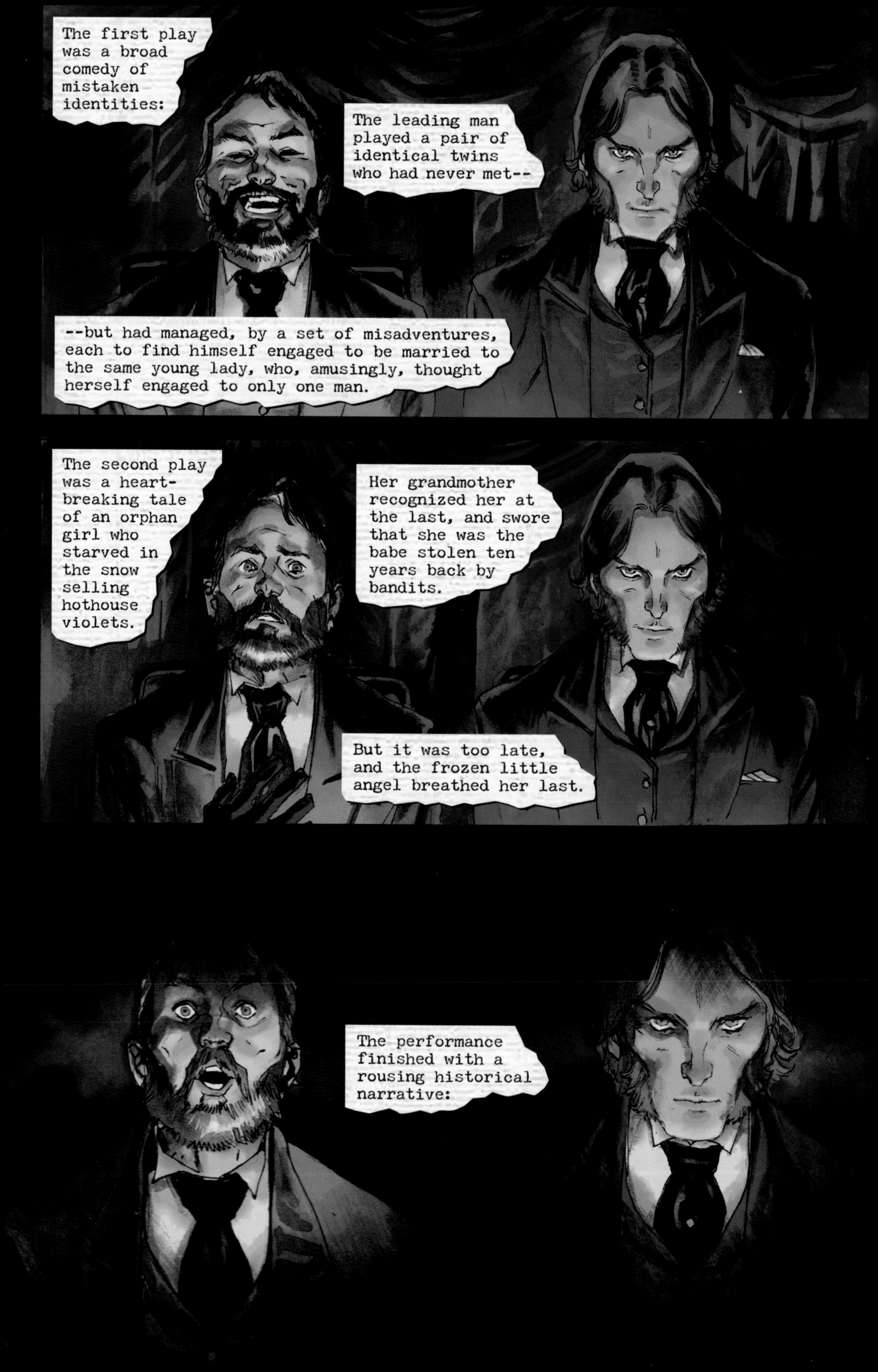
The first play was a broad comedy of mistaken identities:
The leading man played a pair of identical twins who had never met--
--but had managed, by a set of misadventures, each to find himself engaged to be married to the same young lady, who, amusingly, thought herself engaged to only one man.
The second play was a heart-breaking tale of an orphan girl who starved in the snow selling hothouse violets.
Her grandmother recognized her at the last, and swore that she was the babe stolen ten years back by bandits.
But it was too late, and the frozen little angel breathed her last.
The performance finished with a rousing historical narrative:

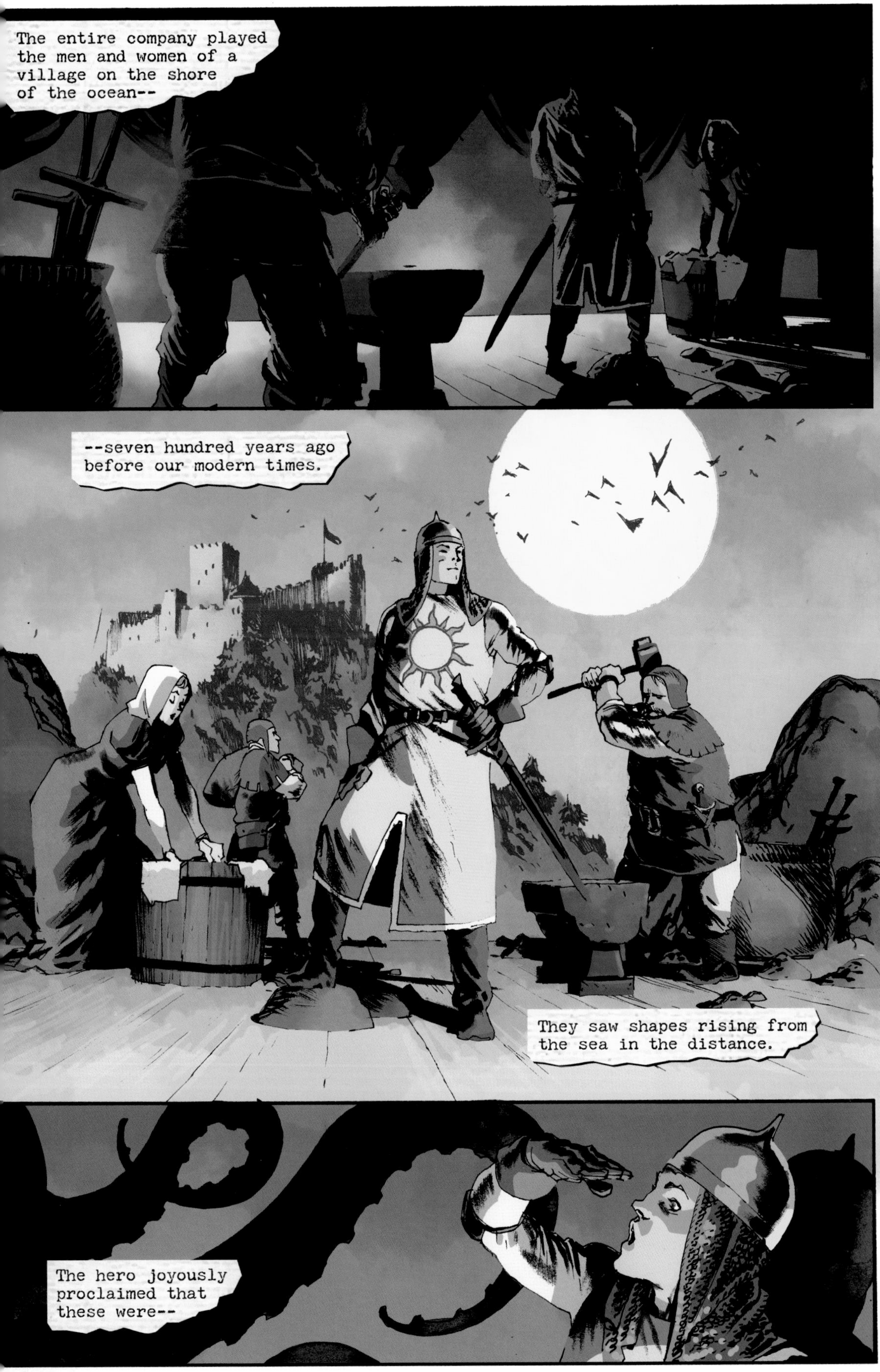
The entire company played the men and women of a village on the shore of the ocean--
--seven hundred years ago before our modern times.
They saw shapes rising from the sea in the distance.
The hero joyously proclaimed that these were--

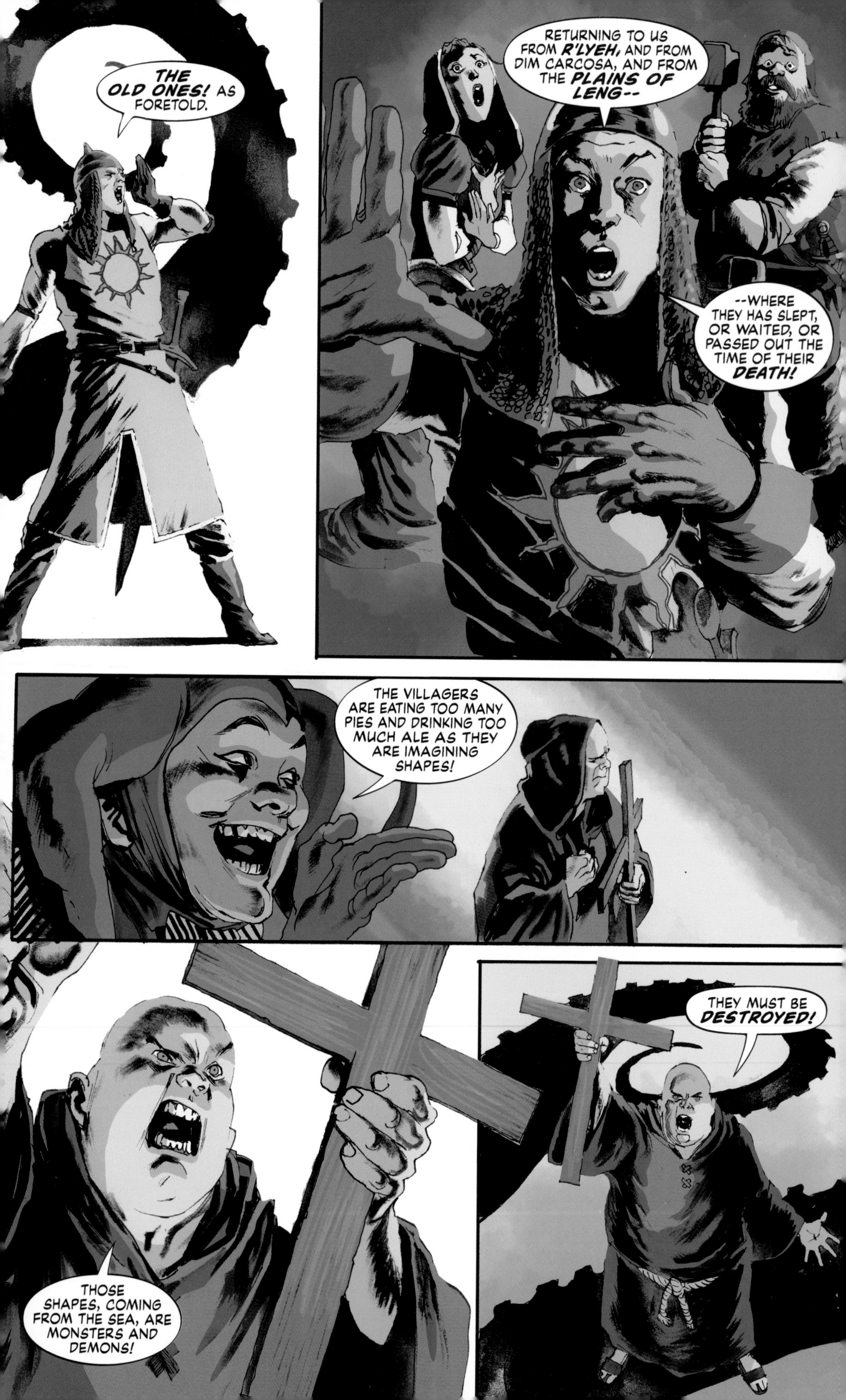
THE OLD ONES! AS FORETOLD.
RETURNING TO US FROM R'LYEH, AND FROM DIM CARCOSA, AND FROM THE PLAINS OF LENG--
--WHERE THEY HAS SLEPT, OR WAITED, OR PASSED OUT THE TIME OF THEIR DEATH!
THE VILLAGERS ARE EATING TOO MANY PIES AND DRINKING TOO MUCH ALE AS THEY ARE IMAGINING SHAPES!
THOSE SHAPES, COMING FROM THE SEA, ARE MONSTERS AND DEMONS!
THEY MUST BE DESTROYED!

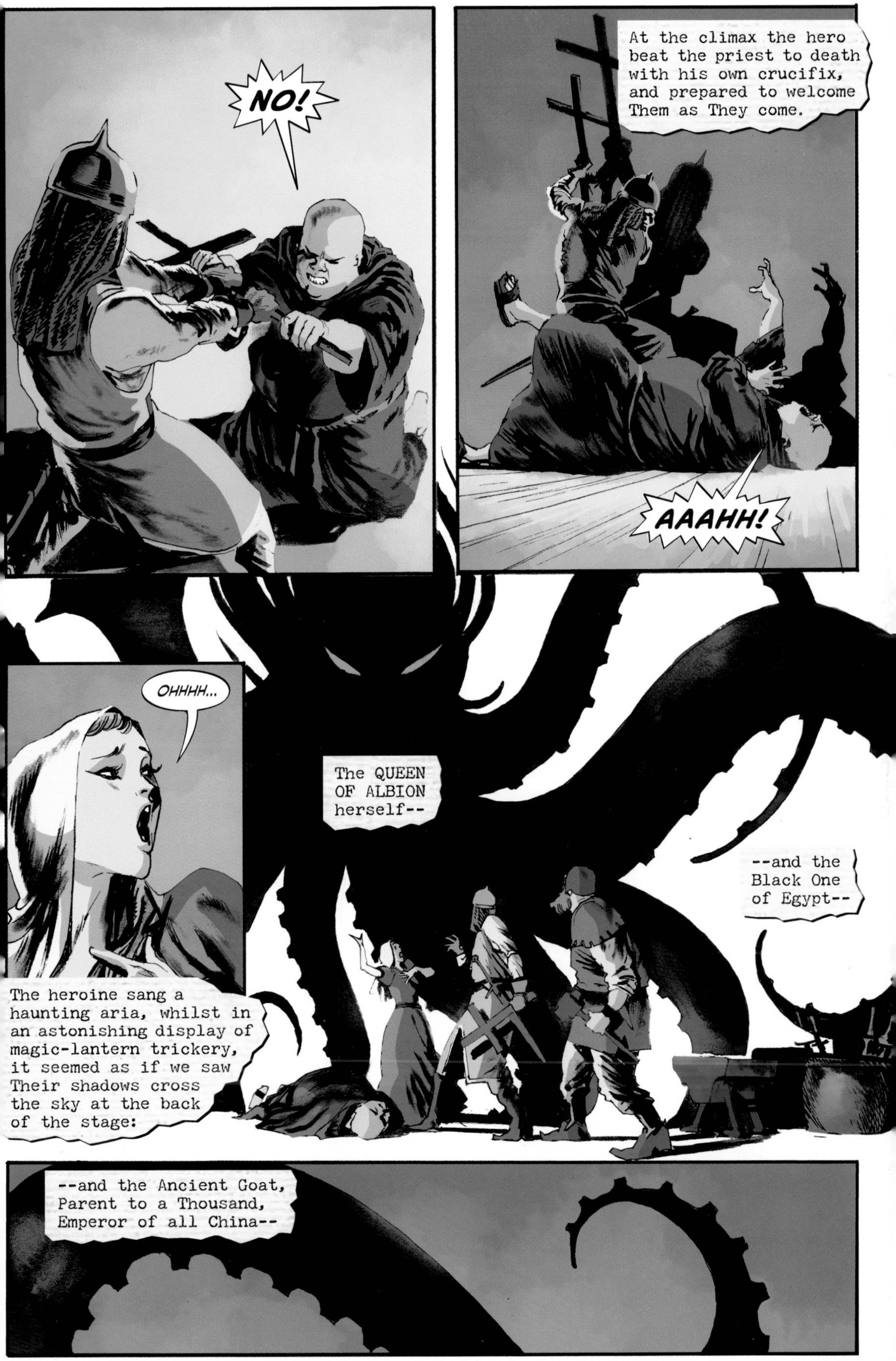
NO!
At the climax the hero beat the priest to death with his own crucifix, and prepared to welcome Them as They come.
AAAHH!
OHHHH...
The heroine sang a haunting aria, whilst in an astonishing display of magic-lantern trickery, it seemed as if we saw Their shadows cross the sky at the back of the stage:
The QUEEN OF ALBION herself--
--and the Black One of Egypt--
--and the Ancient Goat, Parent to a Thousand, Emperor of all China--

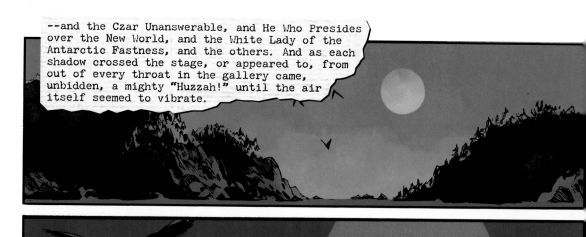

--and the Czar Unanswerable, and He Who Presides over the New World, and the White Lady of the Antarctic Fastness, and the others. And as each shadow crossed the stage, or appeared to, from out of every throat in the gallery came, unbidden, a mighty "Huzzah!" until the air itself seemed to vibrate.

The moon rose in the painted sky, and then, at its height, in one final moment of the theatrical magic, it turned from a pallid yellow, as it was in the old tales, to the comforting crimson of the moon that shines down upon all of us today.

CLAP CLAP CLAP

CLAP CLAP CLAP

CLAP CLAP CLAP CLAP

JOLLY, JOLLY GOOD!

CLAP CLAP CLAP

STOUT FELLOW, LET US GO BACKSTAGE.

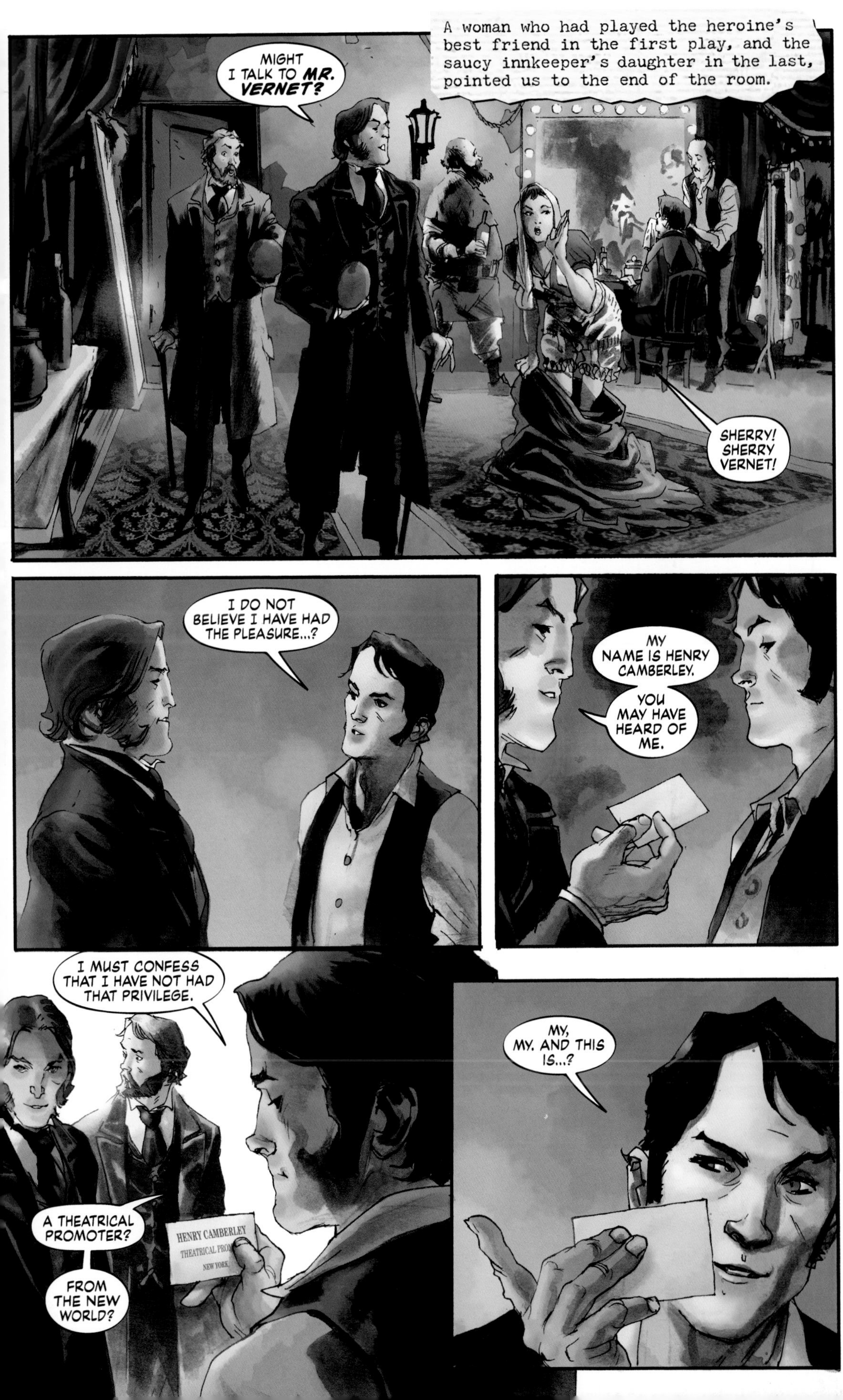

A woman who had played the heroine's best friend in the first play, and the saucy innkeeper's daughter in the last, pointed us to the end of the room.
MIGHT I TALK TO MR. VERNET?
SHERRY! SHERRY VERNET!
I DO NOT BELIEVE I HAVE HAD THE PLEASURE...?
MY NAME IS HENRY CAMBERLEY.
YOU MAY HAVE HEARD OF ME.
I MUST CONFESS THAT I HAVE NOT HAD THAT PRIVILEGE.
A THEATRICAL PROMOTER?
FROM THE NEW WORLD?
HENRY CAMBERLEY
NEW YORK
MY, MY. AND THIS IS...?

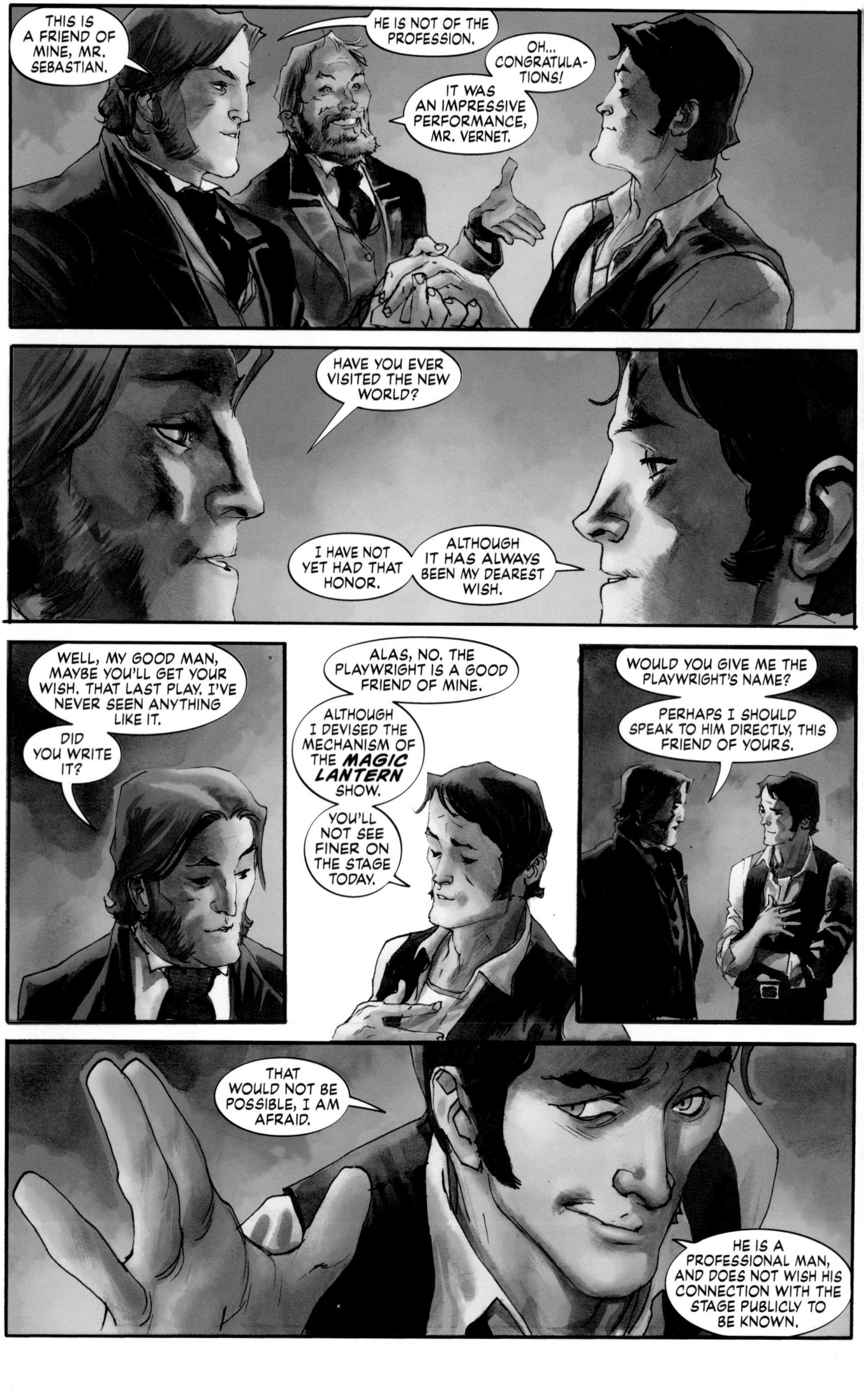
THIS IS A FRIEND OF MINE, MR. SEBASTIAN.
HE IS NOT OF THE PROFESSION.
OH... CONGRATULA-TIONS!
IT WAS AN IMPRESSIVE PERFORMANCE, MR. VERNET.
HAVE YOU EVER VISITED THE NEW WORLD?
I HAVE NOT YET HAD THAT HONOR.
ALTHOUGH IT HAS ALWAYS BEEN MY DEAREST WISH.
WELL, MY GOOD MAN, MAYBE YOU'LL GET YOUR WISH. THAT LAST PLAY. I'VE NEVER SEEN ANYTHING LIKE IT.
DID YOU WRITE IT?
ALAS, NO. THE PLAYWRIGHT IS A GOOD FRIEND OF MINE.
ALTHOUGH I DEVISED THE MECHANISM OF THE ***MAGIC LANTERN*** SHOW.
YOU'LL NOT SEE FINER ON THE STAGE TODAY.
WOULD YOU GIVE ME THE PLAYWRIGHT'S NAME?
PERHAPS I SHOULD SPEAK TO HIM DIRECTLY, THIS FRIEND OF YOURS.
THAT WOULD NOT BE POSSIBLE, I AM AFRAID.
HE IS A PROFESSIONAL MAN, AND DOES NOT WISH HIS CONNECTION WITH THE STAGE PUBLICLY TO BE KNOWN.

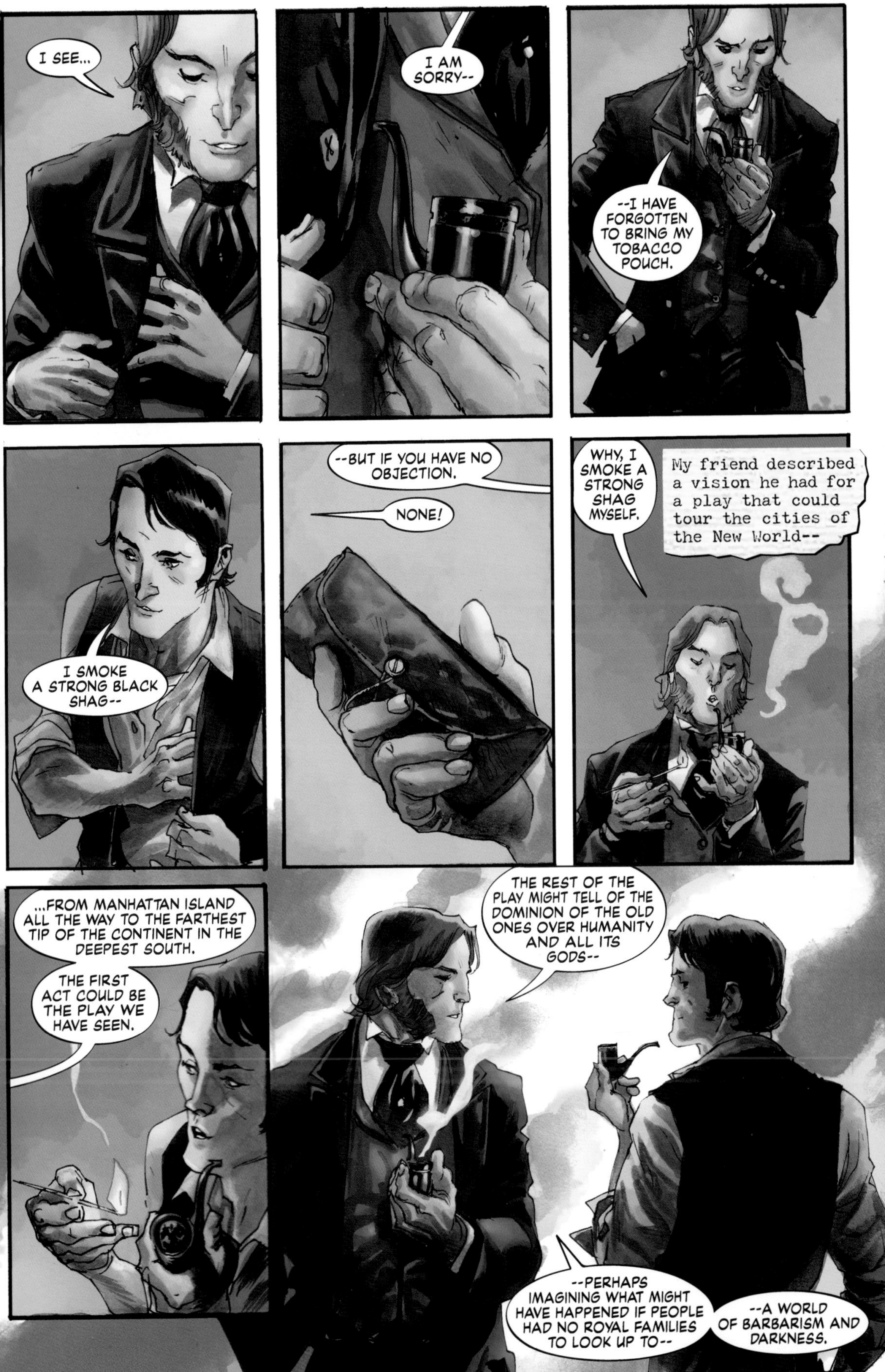
I SEE...
I AM SORRY--
--I HAVE FORGOTTEN TO BRING MY TOBACCO POUCH.
I SMOKE A STRONG BLACK SHAG--
--BUT IF YOU HAVE NO OBJECTION.
NONE!
WHY, I SMOKE A STRONG SHAG MYSELF.
My friend described a vision he had for a play that could tour the cities of the New World--
...FROM MANHATTAN ISLAND ALL THE WAY TO THE FARTHEST TIP OF THE CONTINENT IN THE DEEPEST SOUTH.
THE FIRST ACT COULD BE THE PLAY WE HAVE SEEN.
THE REST OF THE PLAY MIGHT TELL OF THE DOMINION OF THE OLD ONES OVER HUMANITY AND ALL ITS GODS--
--PERHAPS IMAGINING WHAT MIGHT HAVE HAPPENED IF PEOPLE HAD NO ROYAL FAMILIES TO LOOK UP TO--
--A WORLD OF BARBARISM AND DARKNESS.

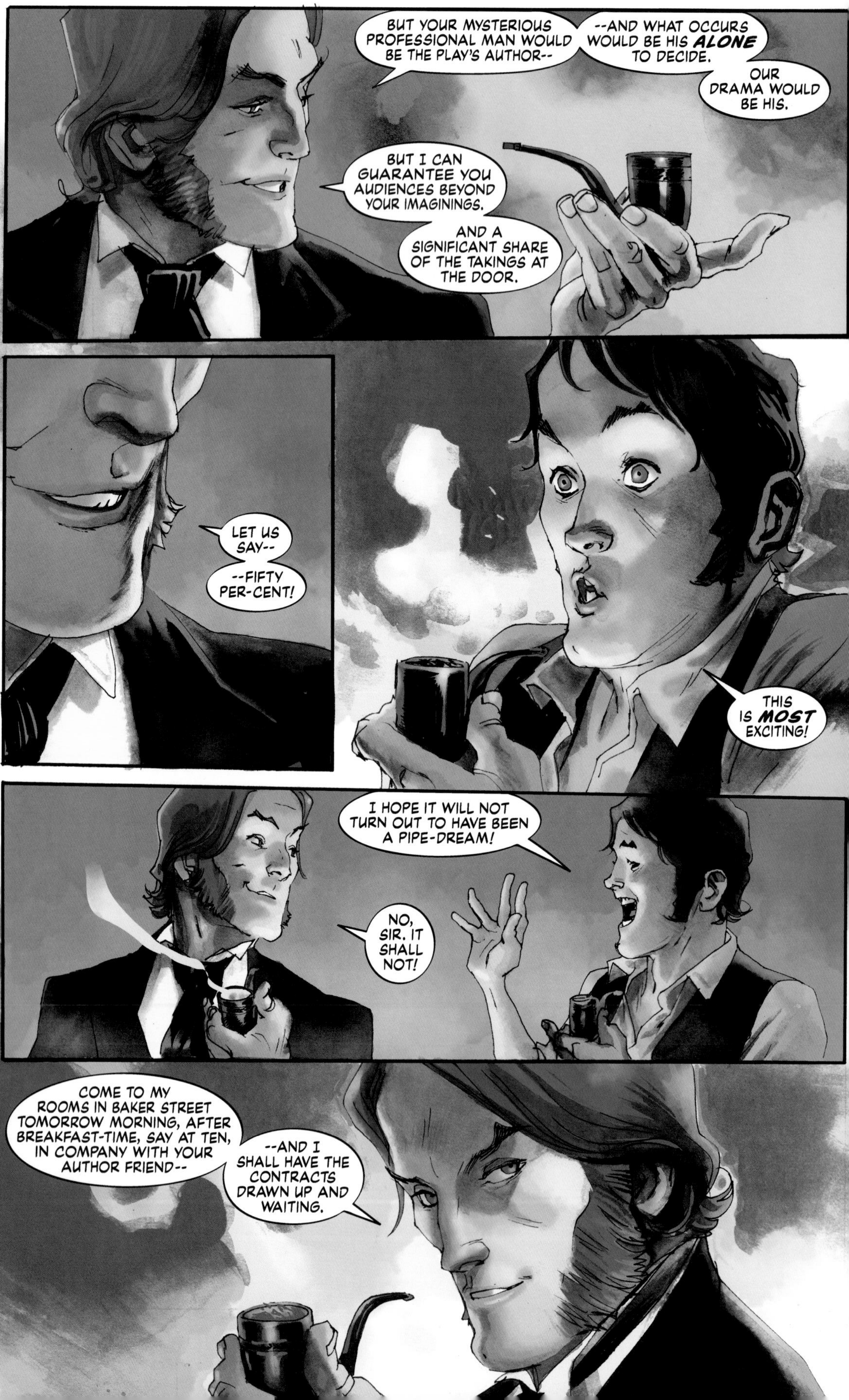
BUT YOUR MYSTERIOUS PROFESSIONAL MAN WOULD BE THE PLAY'S AUTHOR--
--AND WHAT OCCURS WOULD BE HIS ALONE TO DECIDE.
OUR DRAMA WOULD BE HIS.
BUT I CAN GUARANTEE YOU AUDIENCES BEYOND YOUR IMAGININGS.
AND A SIGNIFICANT SHARE OF THE TAKINGS AT THE DOOR.
LET US SAY--
--FIFTY PER-CENT!
THIS IS MOST EXCITING!
I HOPE IT WILL NOT TURN OUT TO HAVE BEEN A PIPE-DREAM!
NO, SIR. IT SHALL NOT!
COME TO MY ROOMS IN BAKER STREET TOMORROW MORNING, AFTER BREAKFAST-TIME, SAY AT TEN, IN COMPANY WITH YOUR AUTHOR FRIEND--
--AND I SHALL HAVE THE CONTRACTS DRAWN UP AND WAITING.

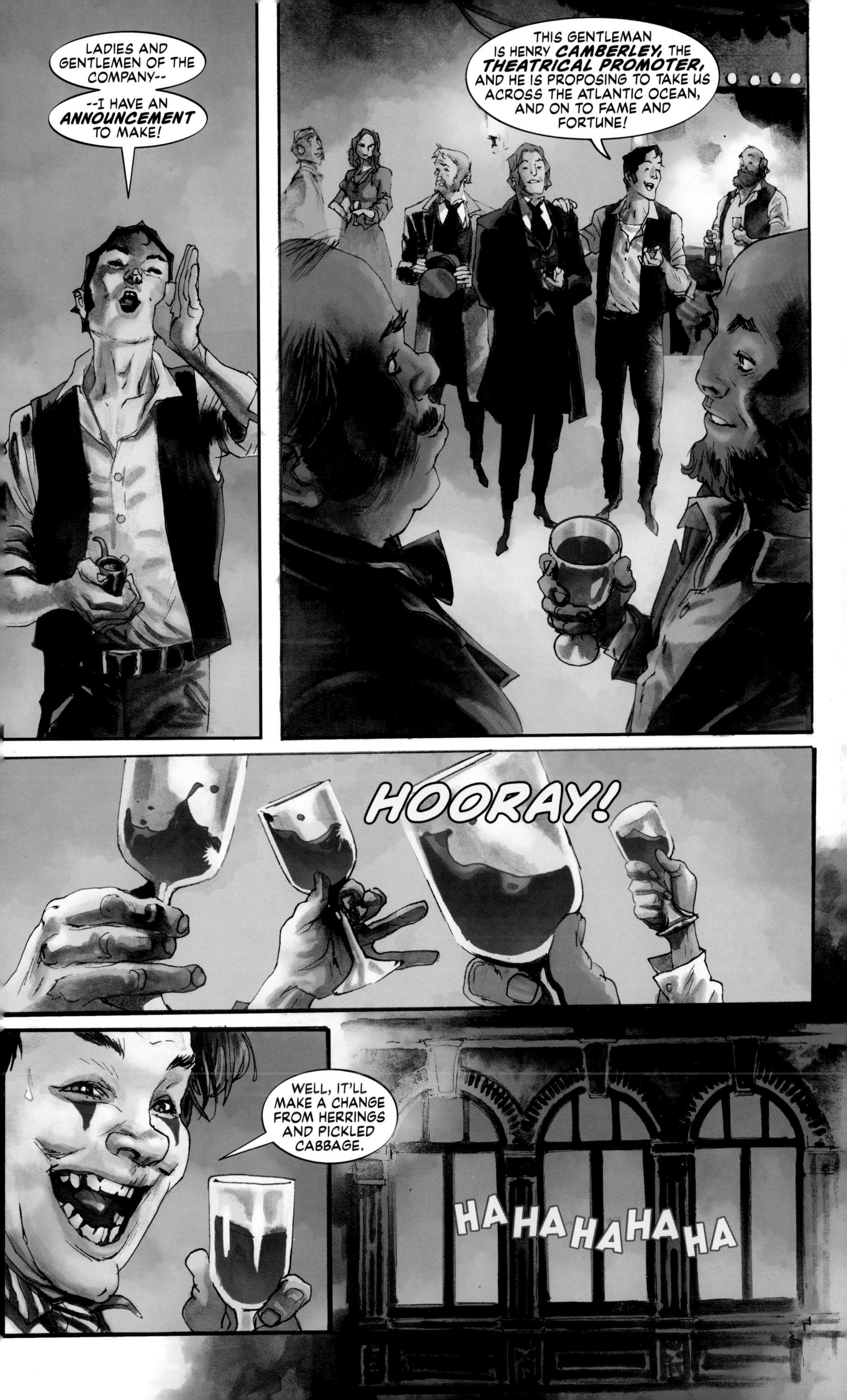
LADIES AND GENTLEMEN OF THE COMPANY--
--I HAVE AN **ANNOUNCEMENT** TO MAKE!
THIS GENTLEMAN IS HENRY **CAMBERLEY,** THE **THEATRICAL PROMOTER,** AND HE IS PROPOSING TO TAKE US ACROSS THE ATLANTIC OCEAN, AND ON TO FAME AND FORTUNE!
HOORAY!
WELL, IT'LL MAKE A CHANGE FROM HERRINGS AND PICKLED CABBAGE.
HAHAHAHAHAHAHA

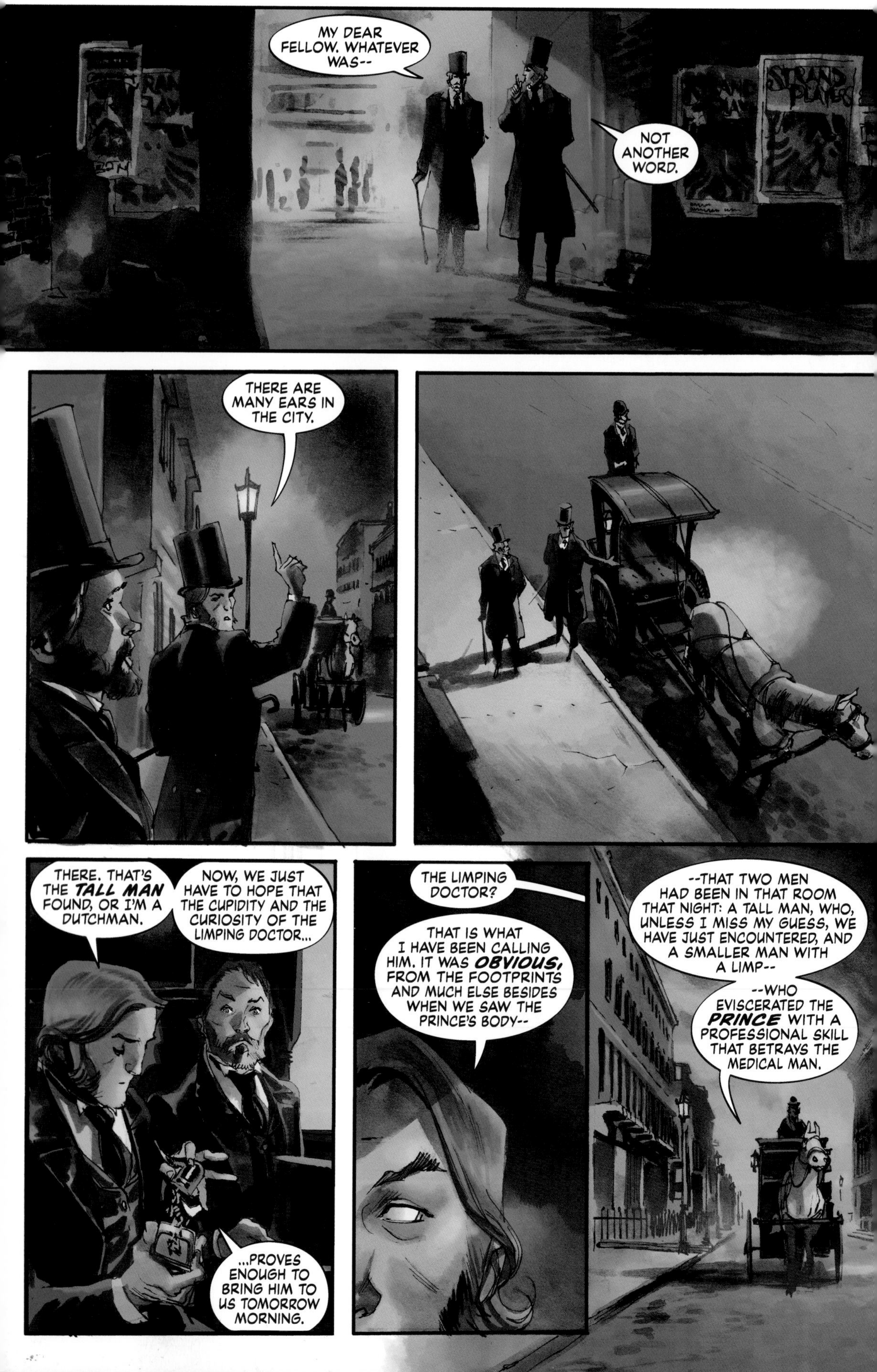
MY DEAR FELLOW. WHATEVER WAS--
STRAND PLAYERS
NOT ANOTHER WORD.
THERE ARE MANY EARS IN THE CITY.
THERE. THAT'S THE **TALL MAN** FOUND, OR I'M A DUTCHMAN.
NOW, WE JUST HAVE TO HOPE THAT THE CUPIDITY AND THE CURIOSITY OF THE LIMPING DOCTOR...
...PROVES ENOUGH TO BRING HIM TO US TOMORROW MORNING.
THE LIMPING DOCTOR?
THAT IS WHAT I HAVE BEEN CALLING HIM. IT WAS **OBVIOUS,** FROM THE FOOTPRINTS AND MUCH ELSE BESIDES WHEN WE SAW THE PRINCE'S BODY--
--THAT TWO MEN HAD BEEN IN THAT ROOM THAT NIGHT: A TALL MAN, WHO, UNLESS I MISS MY GUESS, WE HAVE JUST ENCOUNTERED, AND A SMALLER MAN WITH A LIMP--
--WHO EVISCERATED THE **PRINCE** WITH A PROFESSIONAL SKILL THAT BETRAYS THE MEDICAL MAN.

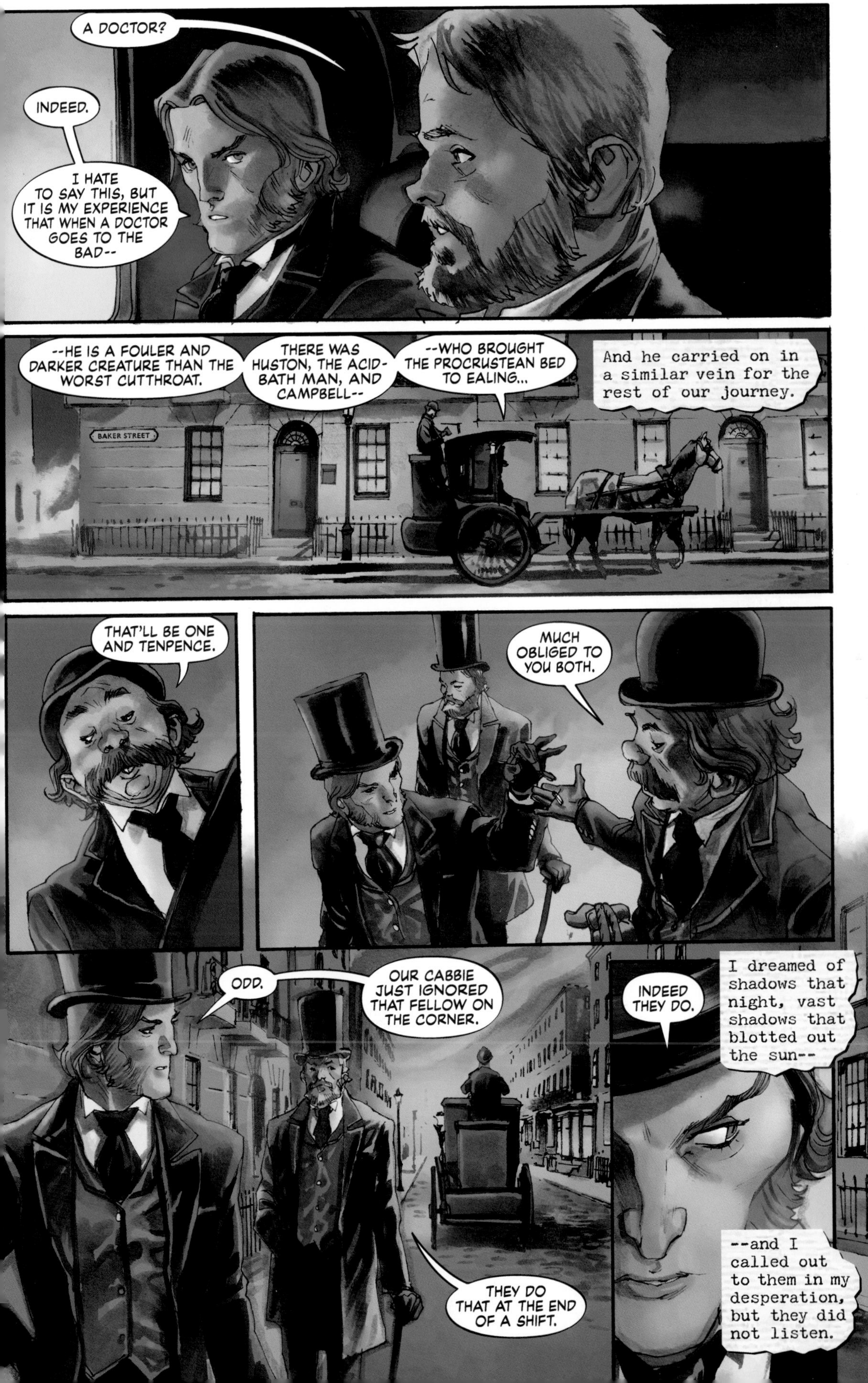
A DOCTOR?
INDEED.
I HATE TO SAY THIS, BUT IT IS MY EXPERIENCE THAT WHEN A DOCTOR GOES TO THE BAD--
--HE IS A FOULER AND DARKER CREATURE THAN THE WORST CUTTHROAT.
THERE WAS HUSTON, THE ACID-BATH MAN, AND CAMPBELL--
--WHO BROUGHT THE PROCRUSTEAN BED TO EALING...
And he carried on in a similar vein for the rest of our journey.
BAKER STREET
THAT'LL BE ONE AND TENPENCE.
MUCH OBLIGED TO YOU BOTH.
ODD.
OUR CABBIE JUST IGNORED THAT FELLOW ON THE CORNER.
THEY DO THAT AT THE END OF A SHIFT.
INDEED THEY DO.
I dreamed of shadows that night, vast shadows that blotted out the sun--
--and I called out to them in my desperation, but they did not listen.

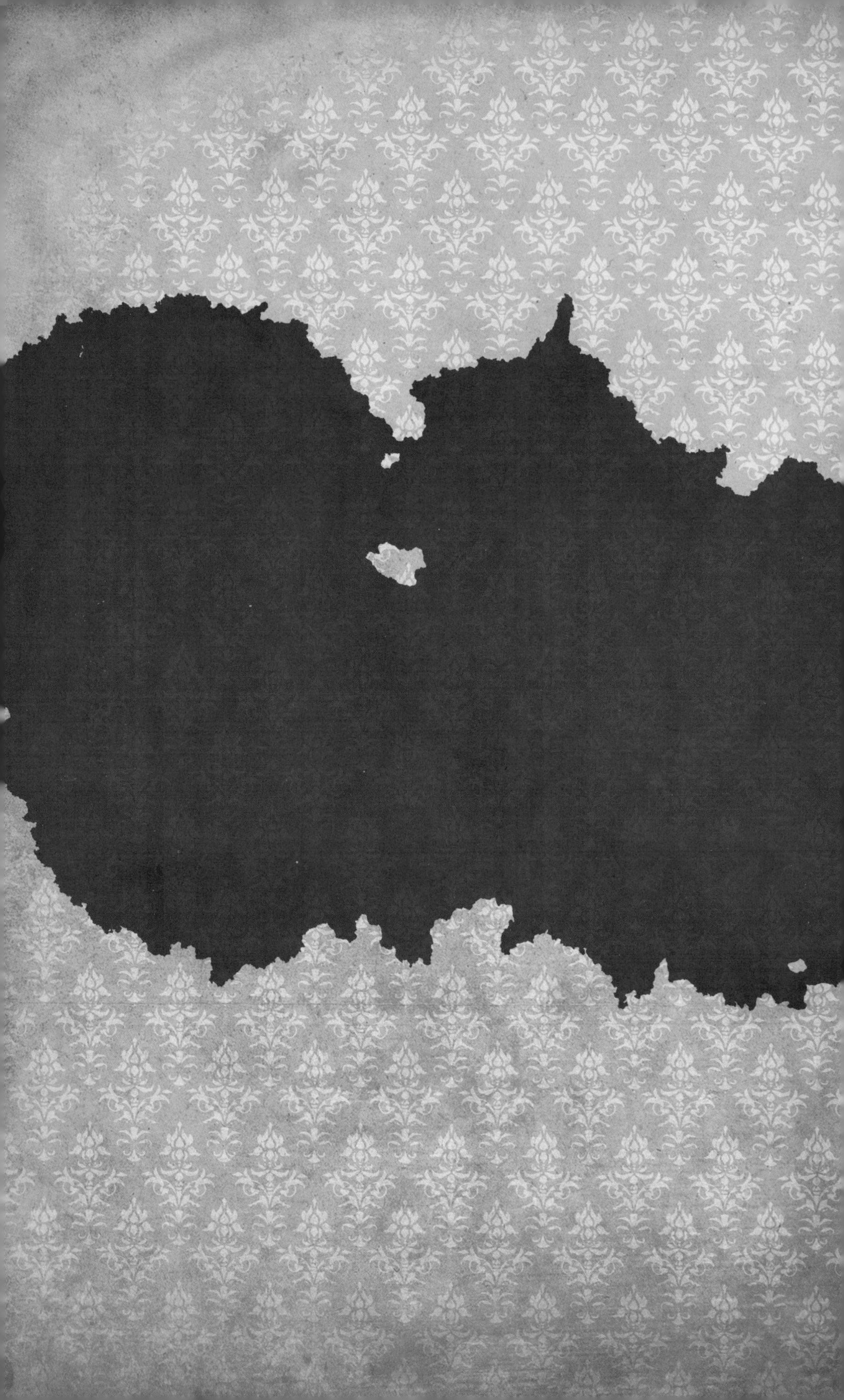

THE SKIN AND
THE PIT

JACK'S

This year, step into the Spring - with a spring in your step! **JACK'S. Boots, Shoes, and Brogues.** Save your soles! Heels our speciality. **JACK'S.** And do not forget to visit our new clothes and fittings emporium in the East End - featuring evening wear of all kinds, hats, novelties, canes, swordsticks &c. **JACK'S OF PICCADILLY.** *It's all in the Spring!*

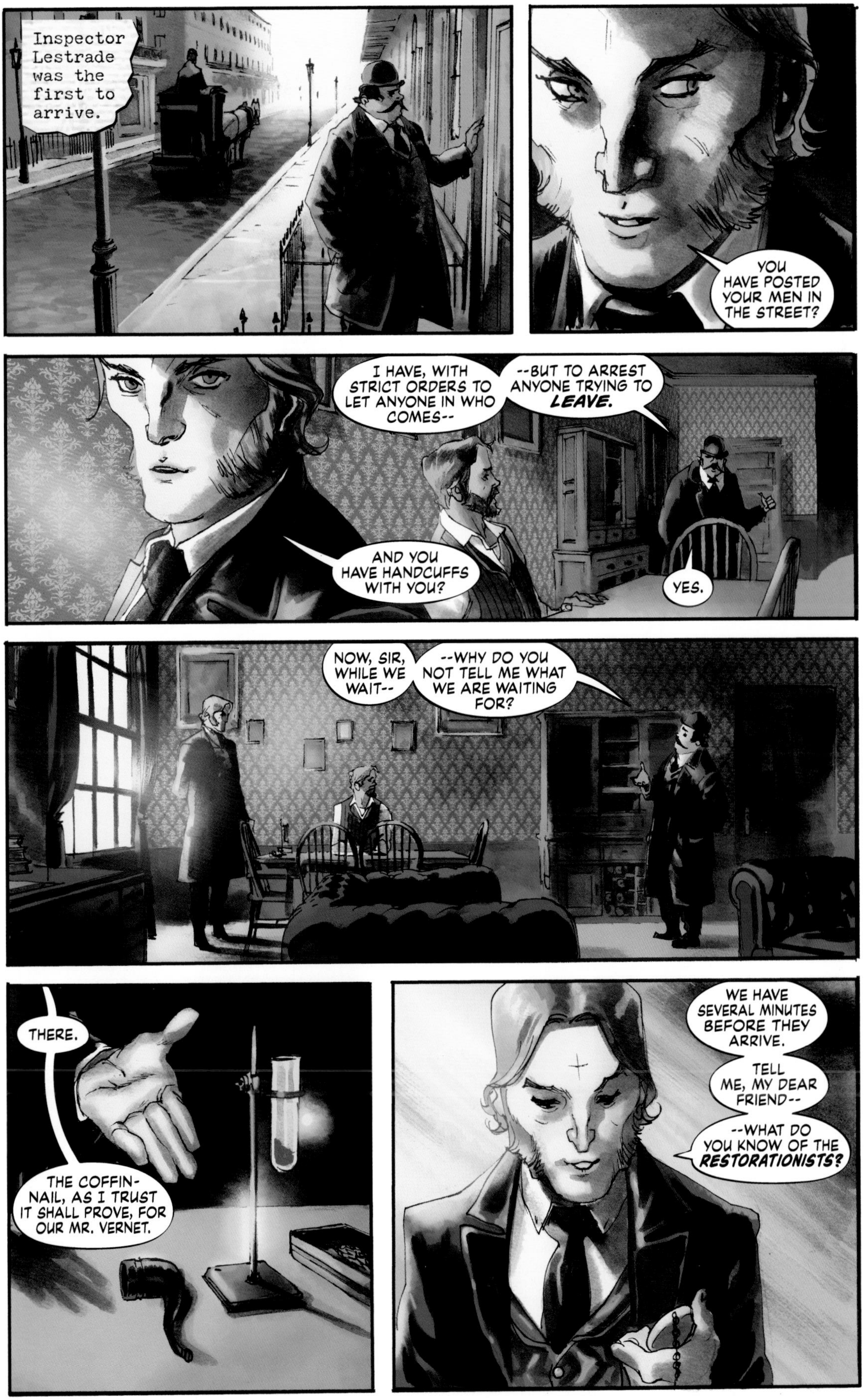
Inspector Lestrade was the first to arrive.
YOU HAVE POSTED YOUR MEN IN THE STREET?
I HAVE, WITH STRICT ORDERS TO LET ANYONE IN WHO COMES--
--BUT TO ARREST ANYONE TRYING TO *LEAVE.*
AND YOU HAVE HANDCUFFS WITH YOU?
YES.
NOW, SIR, WHILE WE WAIT--
--WHY DO YOU NOT TELL ME WHAT WE ARE WAITING FOR?
THERE.
THE COFFIN-NAIL, AS I TRUST IT SHALL PROVE, FOR OUR MR. VERNET.
WE HAVE SEVERAL MINUTES BEFORE THEY ARRIVE.
TELL ME, MY DEAR FRIEND--
--WHAT DO YOU KNOW OF THE ***RESTORATIONISTS?***

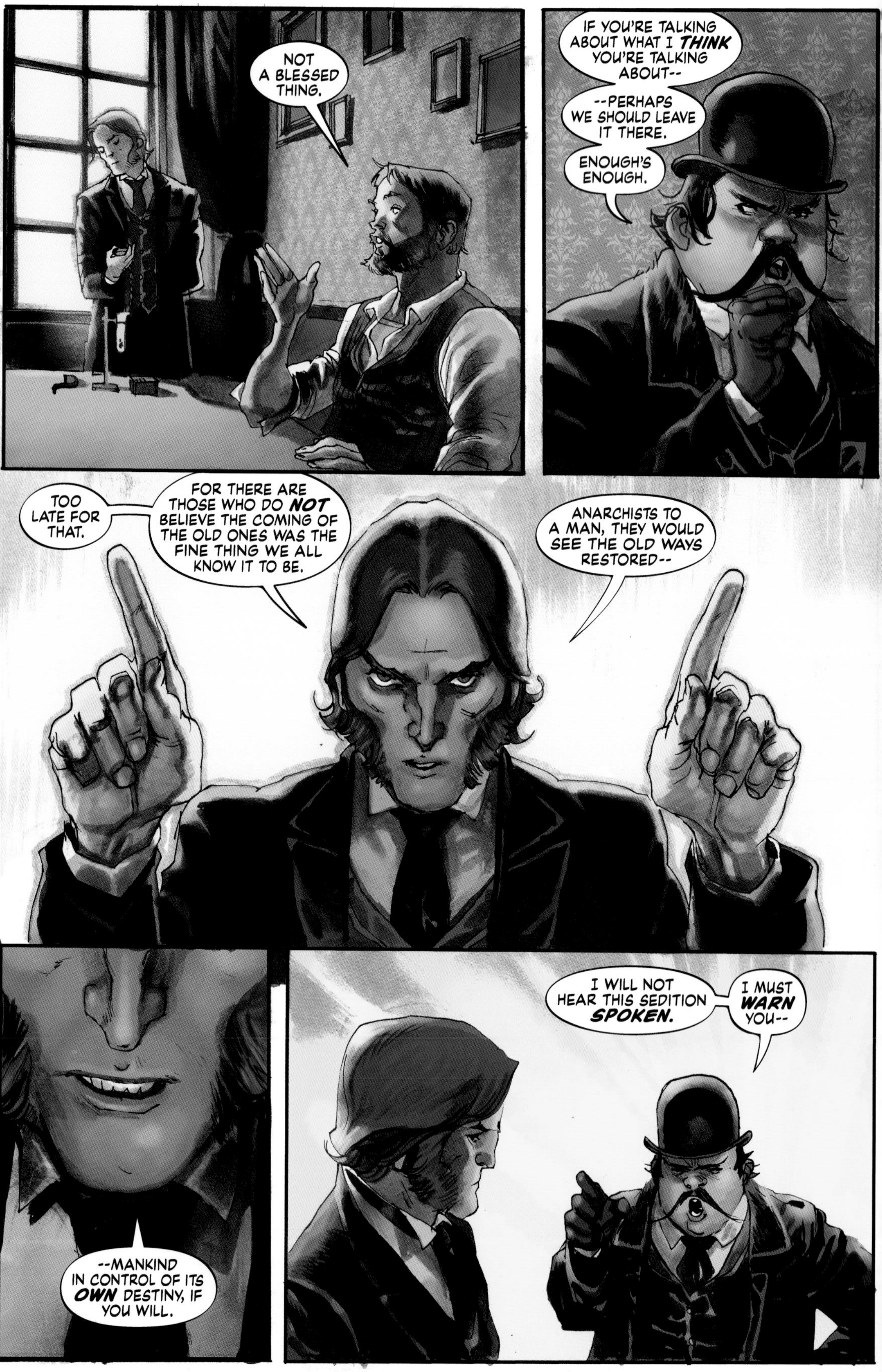
NOT A BLESSED THING.
IF YOU'RE TALKING ABOUT WHAT I *THINK* YOU'RE TALKING ABOUT--
--PERHAPS WE SHOULD LEAVE IT THERE.
ENOUGH'S ENOUGH.
TOO LATE FOR THAT.
FOR THERE ARE THOSE WHO DO *NOT* BELIEVE THE COMING OF THE OLD ONES WAS THE FINE THING WE ALL KNOW IT TO BE.
ANARCHISTS TO A MAN, THEY WOULD SEE THE OLD WAYS RESTORED--
--MANKIND IN CONTROL OF ITS *OWN* DESTINY, IF YOU WILL.
I WILL NOT HEAR THIS SEDITION *SPOKEN.*
I MUST *WARN* YOU--

I MUST WARN *YOU* NOT TO BE SUCH A *FATHEAD*.

BECAUSE IT WAS THE RESTORATIONISTS WHO *KILLED* PRINCE FRANZ DRACO.

THEY MURDER, THEY KILL--

--IN A VAIN EFFORT TO FORCE OUR MASTERS TO LEAVE US ALONE IN THE DARKNESS.

THE PRINCE WAS KILLED BY A *RACHE*--

--AN OLD TERM FOR A HUNTING DOG, INSPECTOR--

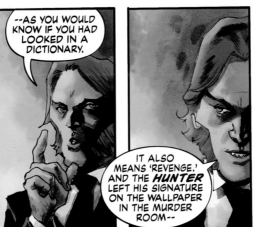

--AS YOU WOULD KNOW IF YOU HAD LOOKED IN A DICTIONARY.

IT ALSO MEANS 'REVENGE.' AND THE *HUNTER* LEFT HIS SIGNATURE ON THE WALLPAPER IN THE MURDER ROOM--

--JUST AS AN ARTIST MIGHT SIGN A CANVAS.

BUT HE WAS *NOT* THE ONE WHO KILLED THE PRINCE.

THE LIMPING *DOCTOR!*

VERY GOOD.

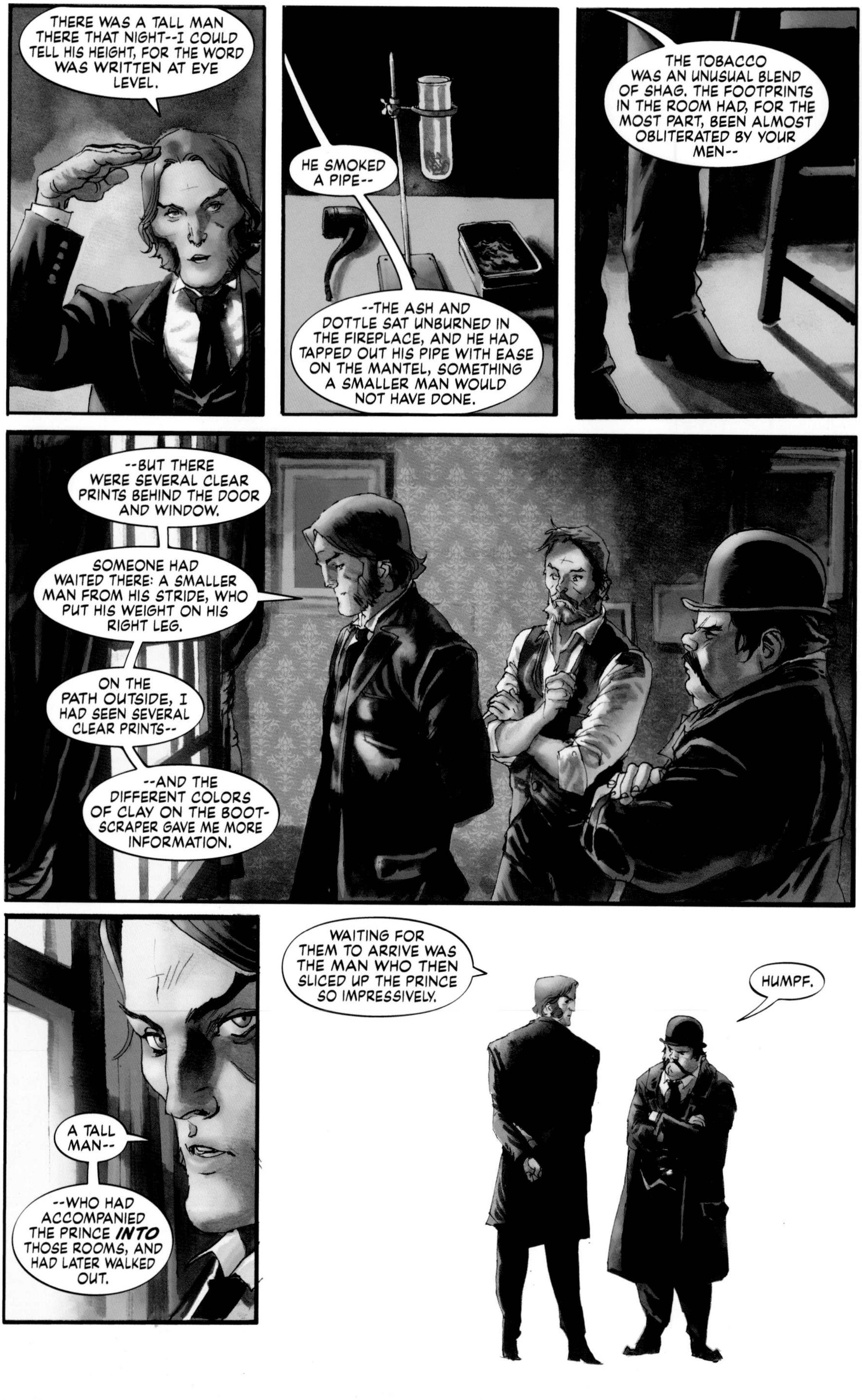
THERE WAS A TALL MAN THERE THAT NIGHT--I COULD TELL HIS HEIGHT, FOR THE WORD WAS WRITTEN AT EYE LEVEL.
HE SMOKED A PIPE--
--THE ASH AND DOTTLE SAT UNBURNED IN THE FIREPLACE, AND HE HAD TAPPED OUT HIS PIPE WITH EASE ON THE MANTEL, SOMETHING A SMALLER MAN WOULD NOT HAVE DONE.
THE TOBACCO WAS AN UNUSUAL BLEND OF SHAG. THE FOOTPRINTS IN THE ROOM HAD, FOR THE MOST PART, BEEN ALMOST OBLITERATED BY YOUR MEN--
--BUT THERE WERE SEVERAL CLEAR PRINTS BEHIND THE DOOR AND WINDOW.
SOMEONE HAD WAITED THERE: A SMALLER MAN FROM HIS STRIDE, WHO PUT HIS WEIGHT ON HIS RIGHT LEG.
ON THE PATH OUTSIDE, I HAD SEEN SEVERAL CLEAR PRINTS--
--AND THE DIFFERENT COLORS OF CLAY ON THE BOOT-SCRAPER GAVE ME MORE INFORMATION.
A TALL MAN--
--WHO HAD ACCOMPANIED THE PRINCE ***INTO*** THOSE ROOMS, AND HAD LATER WALKED OUT.
WAITING FOR THEM TO ARRIVE WAS THE MAN WHO THEN SLICED UP THE PRINCE SO IMPRESSIVELY.
HUMPF.

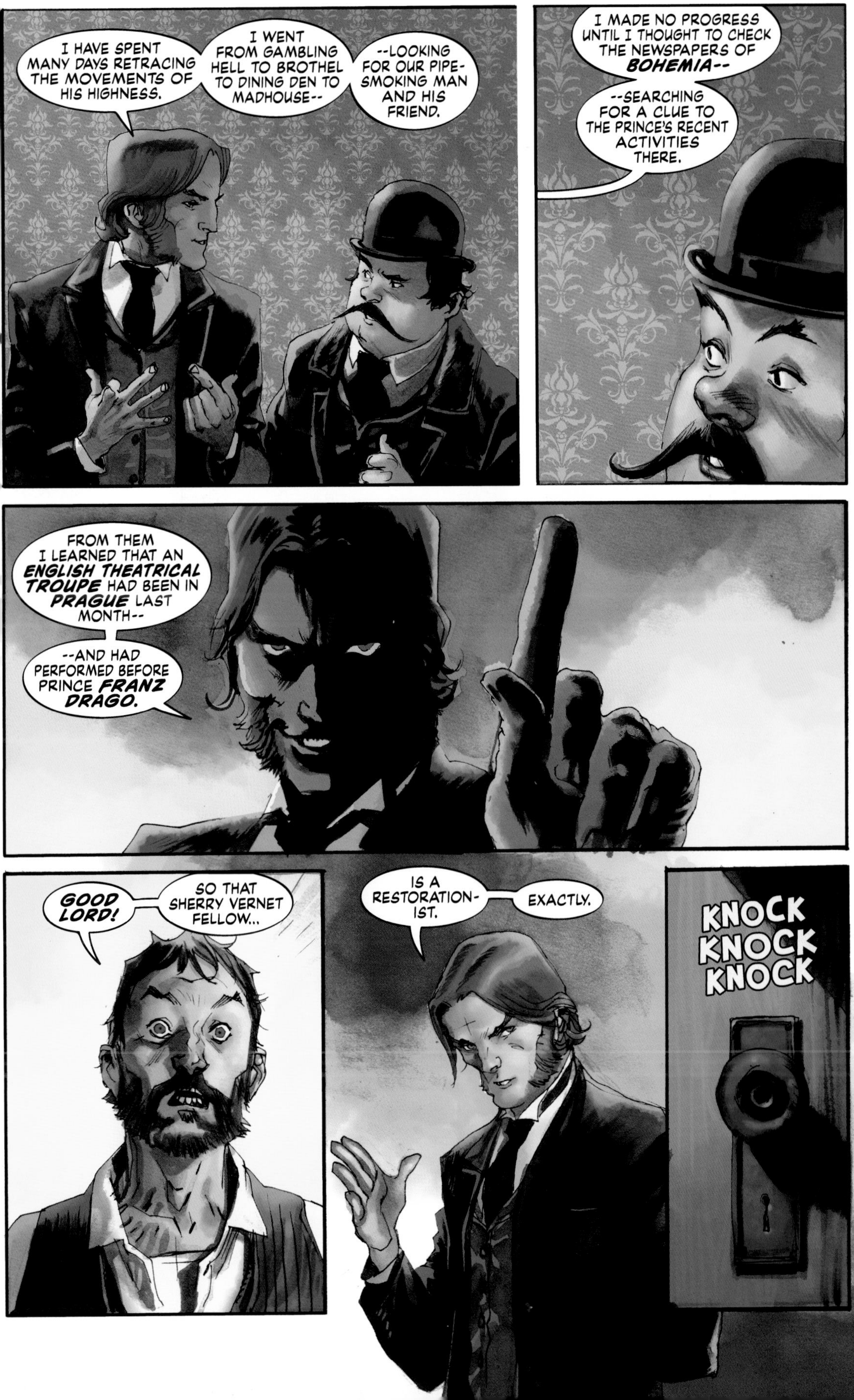
I HAVE SPENT MANY DAYS RETRACING THE MOVEMENTS OF HIS HIGHNESS.
I WENT FROM GAMBLING HELL TO BROTHEL TO DINING DEN TO MADHOUSE--
--LOOKING FOR OUR PIPE-SMOKING MAN AND HIS FRIEND.
I MADE NO PROGRESS UNTIL I THOUGHT TO CHECK THE NEWSPAPERS OF BOHEMIA--
--SEARCHING FOR A CLUE TO THE PRINCE'S RECENT ACTIVITIES THERE.
FROM THEM I LEARNED THAT AN ENGLISH THEATRICAL TROUPE HAD BEEN IN PRAGUE LAST MONTH--
--AND HAD PERFORMED BEFORE PRINCE FRANZ DRAGO.
GOOD LORD!
SO THAT SHERRY VERNET FELLOW...
IS A RESTORATION-IST.
EXACTLY.
KNOCK KNOCK KNOCK

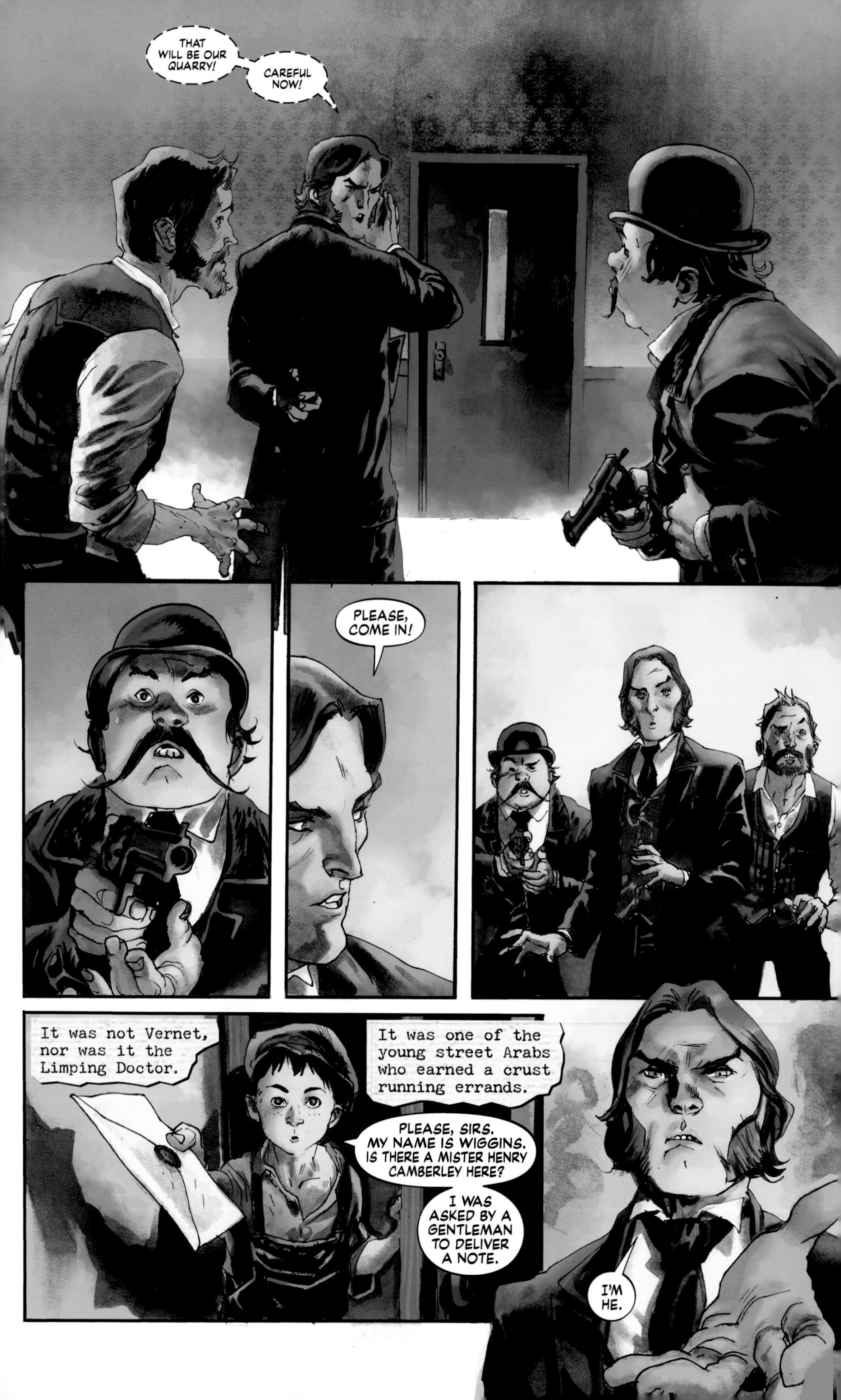

THAT WILL BE OUR QUARRY!
CAREFUL NOW!
PLEASE, COME IN!
It was not Vernet, nor was it the Limping Doctor.
It was one of the young street Arabs who earned a crust running errands.
PLEASE, SIRS. MY NAME IS WIGGINS. IS THERE A MISTER HENRY CAMBERLEY HERE?
I WAS ASKED BY A GENTLEMAN TO DELIVER A NOTE.
I'M HE.

My Dear Sir,

I do not address you as Henry Camberley, for it is a name to which you have no claim.

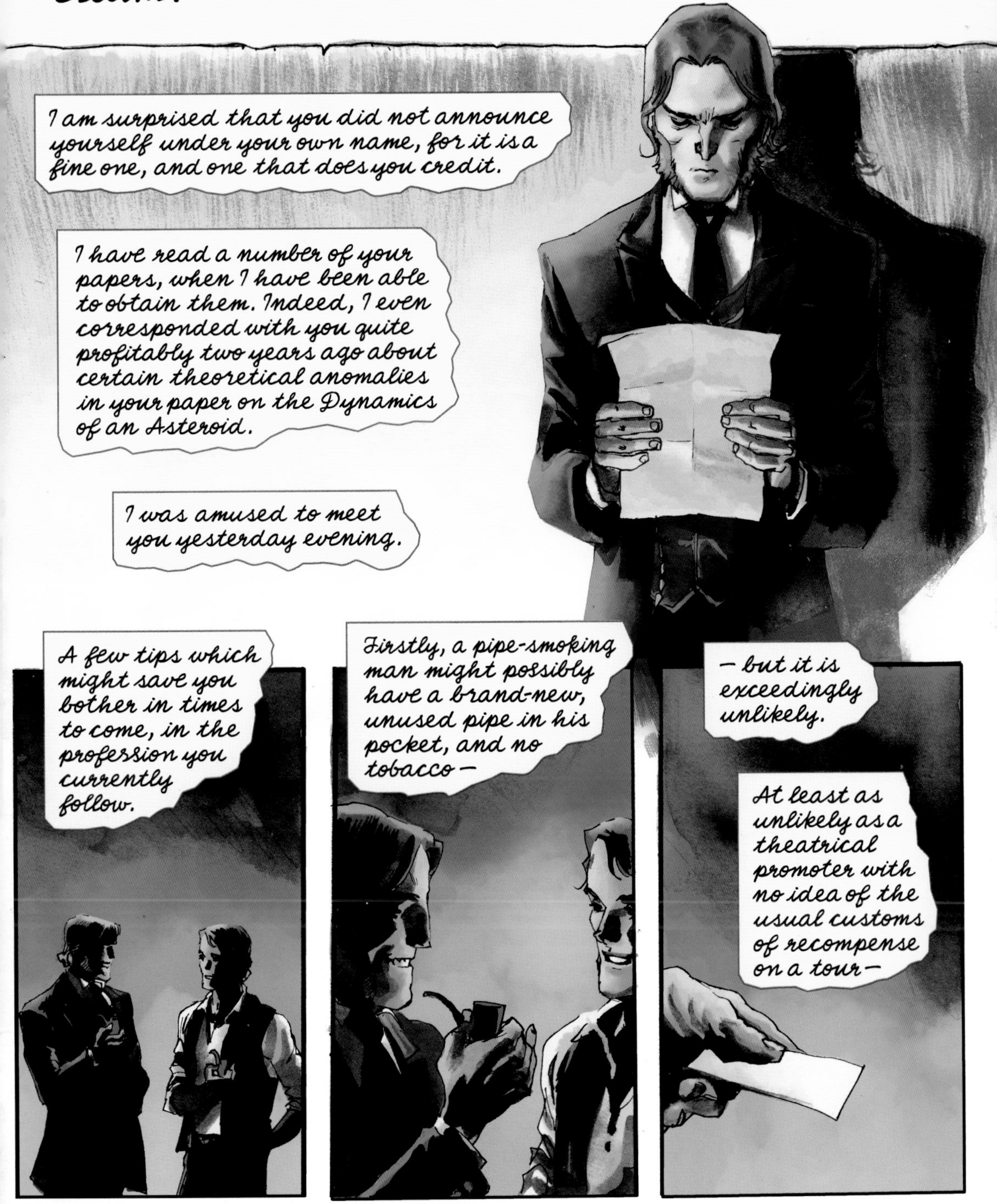

I am surprised that you did not announce yourself under your own name, for it is a fine one, and one that does you credit.
I have read a number of your papers, when I have been able to obtain them. Indeed, I even corresponded with you quite profitably two years ago about certain theoretical anomalies in your paper on the Dynamics of an Asteroid.
I was amused to meet you yesterday evening.
A few tips which might save you bother in times to come, in the profession you currently follow.
Firstly, a pipe-smoking man might possibly have a brand-new, unused pipe in his pocket, and no tobacco—
—but it is exceedingly unlikely.
At least as unlikely as a theatrical promoter with no idea of the usual customs of recompense on a tour—

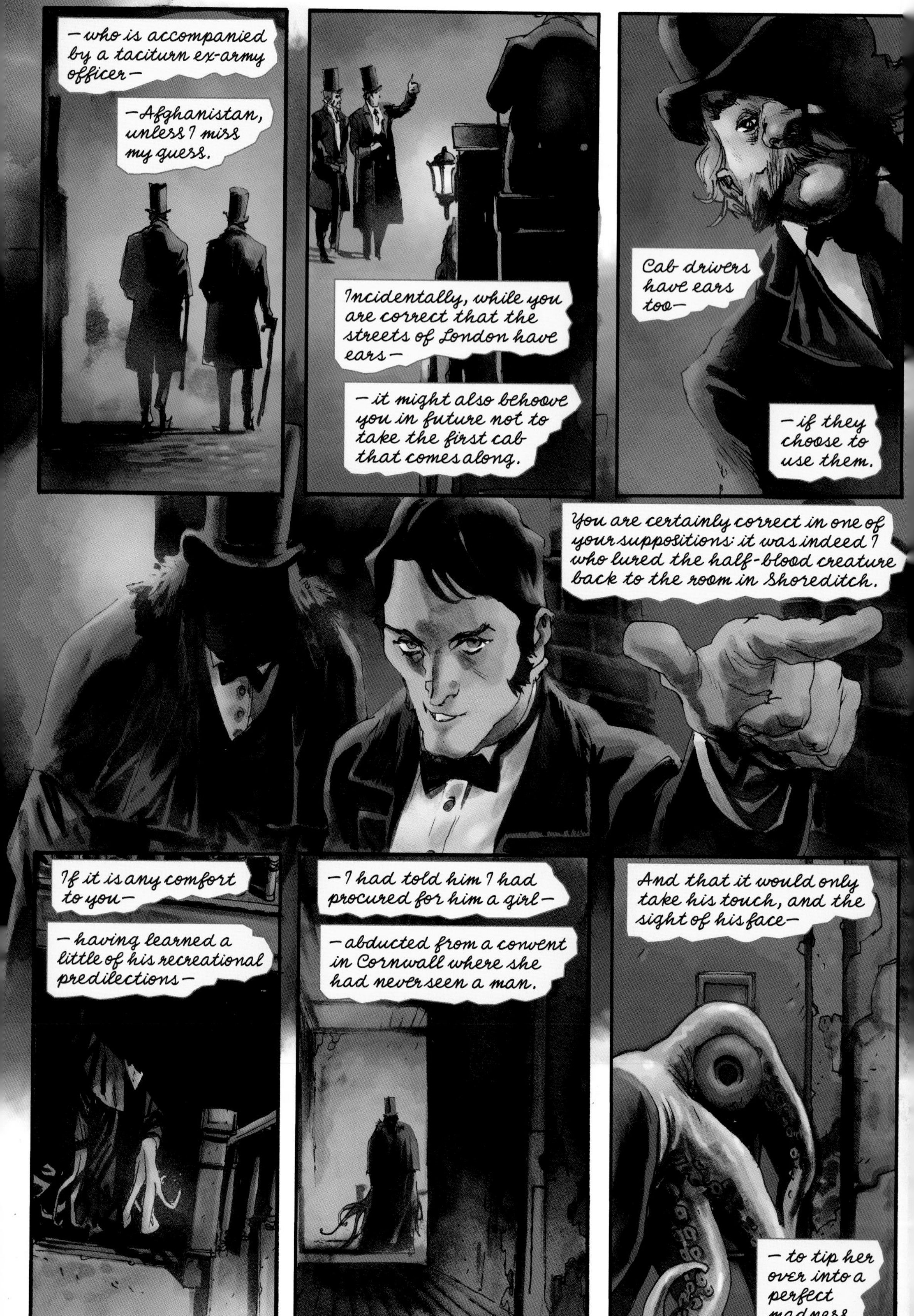
—who is accompanied by a taciturn ex-army officer—
—Afghanistan, unless I miss my guess.
Incidentally, while you are correct that the streets of London have ears—
—it might also behoove you in future not to take the first cab that comes along.
Cab drivers have ears too—
—if they choose to use them.
You are certainly correct in one of your suppositions: it was indeed I who lured the half-blood creature back to the room in Shoreditch.
If it is any comfort to you—
—having learned a little of his recreational predilections—
—I had told him I had procured for him a girl—
—abducted from a convent in Cornwall where she had never seen a man.
And that it would only take his touch, and the sight of his face—
—to tip her over into a perfect madness.

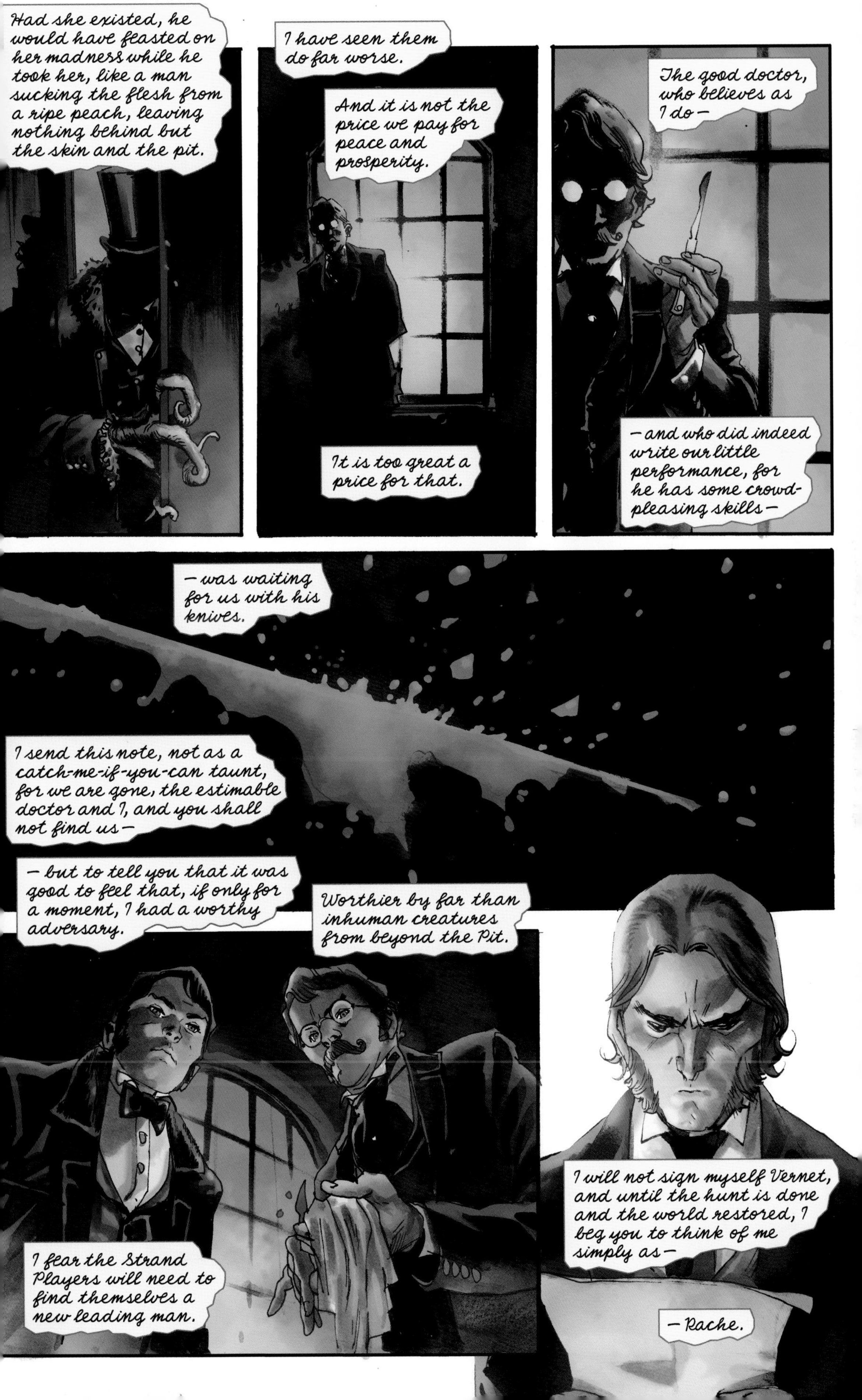
Had she existed, he would have feasted on her madness while he took her, like a man sucking the flesh from a ripe peach, leaving nothing behind but the skin and the pit.
I have seen them do far worse.
And it is not the price we pay for peace and prosperity.
It is too great a price for that.
The good doctor, who believes as I do—
—and who did indeed write our little performance, for he has some crowd-pleasing skills—
—was waiting for us with his knives.
I send this note, not as a catch-me-if-you-can taunt, for we are gone, the estimable doctor and I, and you shall not find us—
—but to tell you that it was good to feel that, if only for a moment, I had a worthy adversary.
Worthier by far than inhuman creatures from beyond the Pit.
I fear the Strand Players will need to find themselves a new leading man.
I will not sign myself Vernet, and until the hunt is done and the world restored, I beg you to think of me simply as—
—Rache.

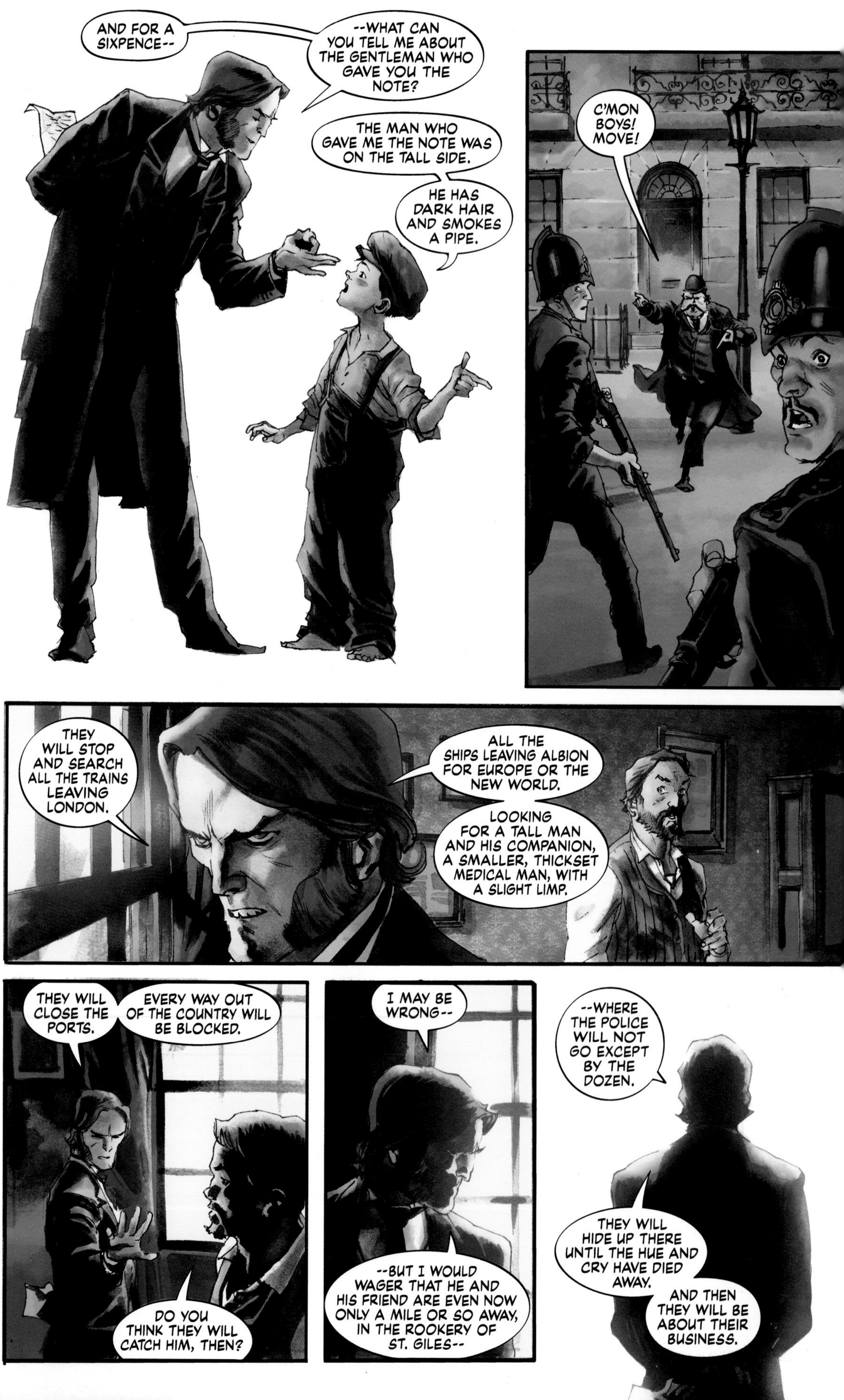
AND FOR A SIXPENCE--
--WHAT CAN YOU TELL ME ABOUT THE GENTLEMAN WHO GAVE YOU THE NOTE?
THE MAN WHO GAVE ME THE NOTE WAS ON THE TALL SIDE.
HE HAS DARK HAIR AND SMOKES A PIPE.
C'MON BOYS! MOVE!
THEY WILL STOP AND SEARCH ALL THE TRAINS LEAVING LONDON.
ALL THE SHIPS LEAVING ALBION FOR EUROPE OR THE NEW WORLD.
LOOKING FOR A TALL MAN AND HIS COMPANION, A SMALLER, THICKSET MEDICAL MAN, WITH A SLIGHT LIMP.
THEY WILL CLOSE THE PORTS.
EVERY WAY OUT OF THE COUNTRY WILL BE BLOCKED.
DO YOU THINK THEY WILL CATCH HIM, THEN?
I MAY BE WRONG--
--BUT I WOULD WAGER THAT HE AND HIS FRIEND ARE EVEN NOW ONLY A MILE OR SO AWAY, IN THE ROOKERY OF ST. GILES--
--WHERE THE POLICE WILL NOT GO EXCEPT BY THE DOZEN.
THEY WILL HIDE UP THERE UNTIL THE HUE AND CRY HAVE DIED AWAY.
AND THEN THEY WILL BE ABOUT THEIR BUSINESS.

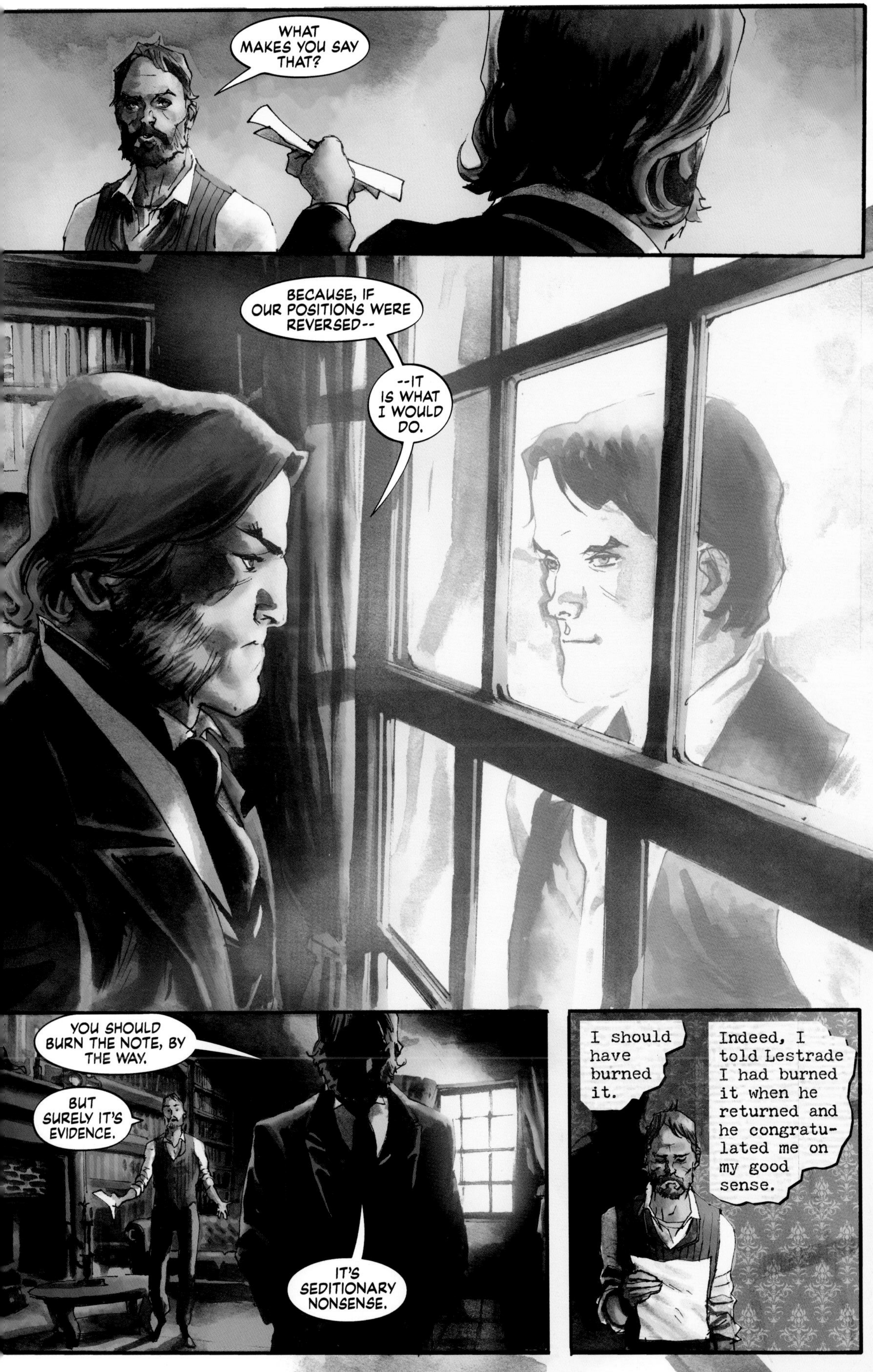
WHAT MAKES YOU SAY THAT?
BECAUSE, IF OUR POSITIONS WERE REVERSED--
--IT IS WHAT I WOULD DO.
YOU SHOULD BURN THE NOTE, BY THE WAY.
BUT SURELY IT'S EVIDENCE.
IT'S SEDITIONARY NONSENSE.
I should have burned it.
Indeed, I told Lestrade I had burned it when he returned and he congratulated me on my good sense.

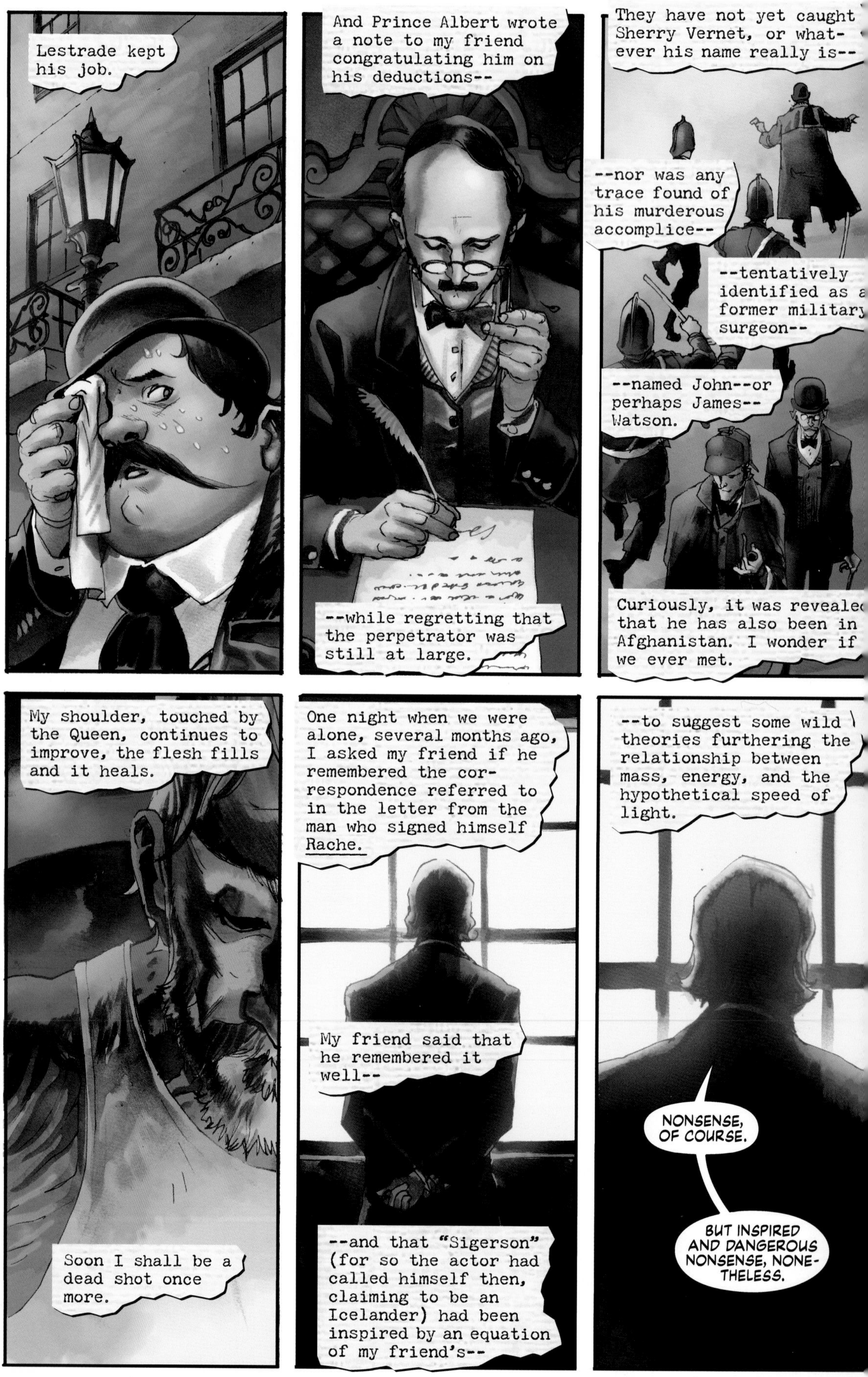
Lestrade kept his job.
And Prince Albert wrote a note to my friend congratulating him on his deductions--
--while regretting that the perpetrator was still at large.
They have not yet caught Sherry Vernet, or whatever his name really is--
--nor was any trace found of his murderous accomplice--
--tentatively identified as a former military surgeon--
--named John--or perhaps James--Watson.
Curiously, it was revealed that he has also been in Afghanistan. I wonder if we ever met.
My shoulder, touched by the Queen, continues to improve, the flesh fills and it heals.
Soon I shall be a dead shot once more.
One night when we were alone, several months ago, I asked my friend if he remembered the correspondence referred to in the letter from the man who signed himself Rache.
My friend said that he remembered it well--
--and that "Sigerson" (for so the actor had called himself then, claiming to be an Icelander) had been inspired by an equation of my friend's--
--to suggest some wild theories furthering the relationship between mass, energy, and the hypothetical speed of light.
NONSENSE, OF COURSE.
BUT INSPIRED AND DANGEROUS NONSENSE, NONETHELESS.

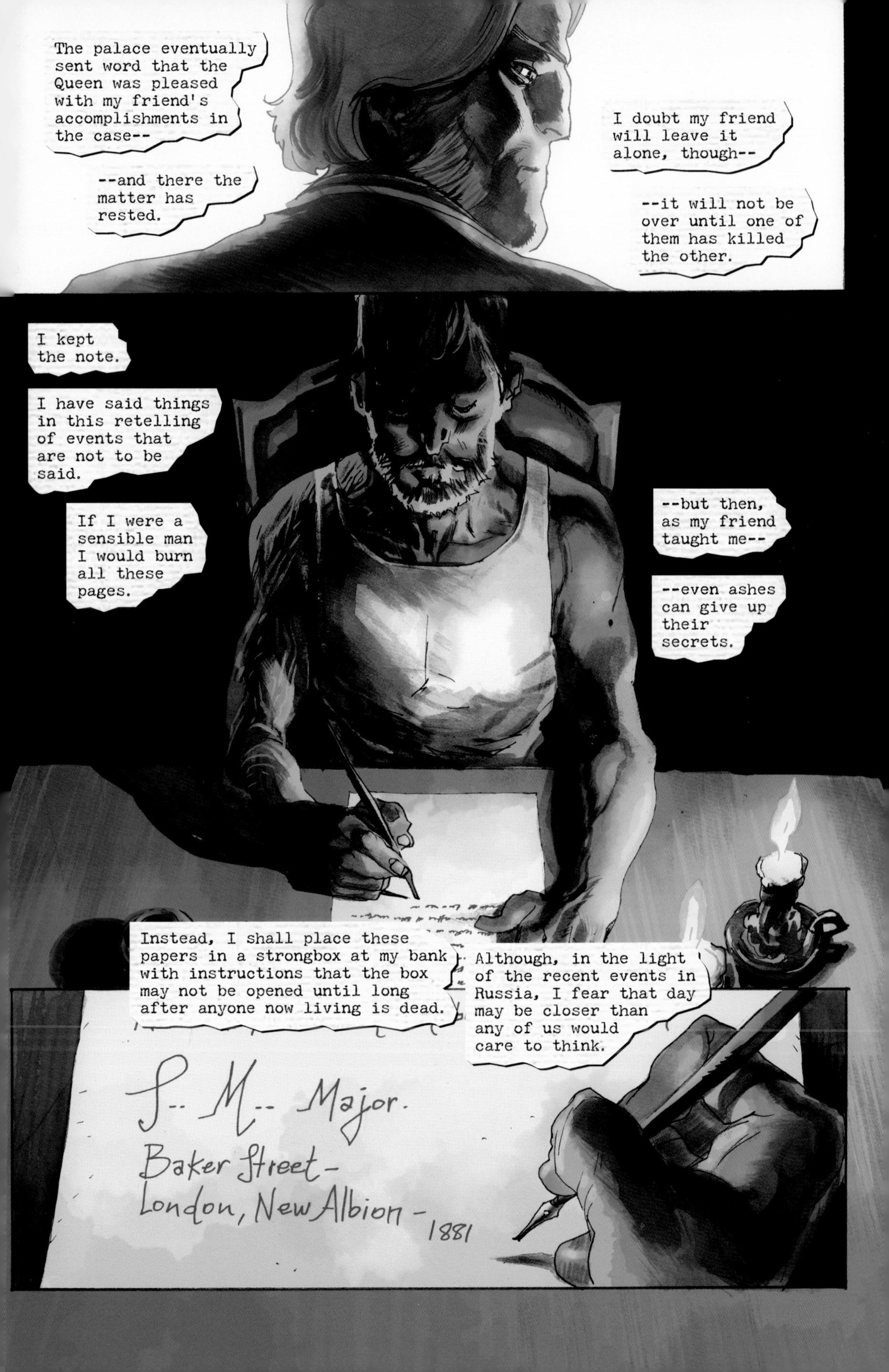
The palace eventually sent word that the Queen was pleased with my friend's accomplishments in the case--
--and there the matter has rested.
I doubt my friend will leave it alone, though--
--it will not be over until one of them has killed the other.
I kept the note.
I have said things in this retelling of events that are not to be said.
If I were a sensible man I would burn all these pages.
--but then, as my friend taught me--
--even ashes can give up their secrets.
Instead, I shall place these papers in a strongbox at my bank with instructions that the box may not be opened until long after anyone now living is dead.
Although, in the light of the recent events in Russia, I fear that day may be closer than any of us would care to think.
S-- M-- Major.
Baker Street-
London, New Albion-
1881

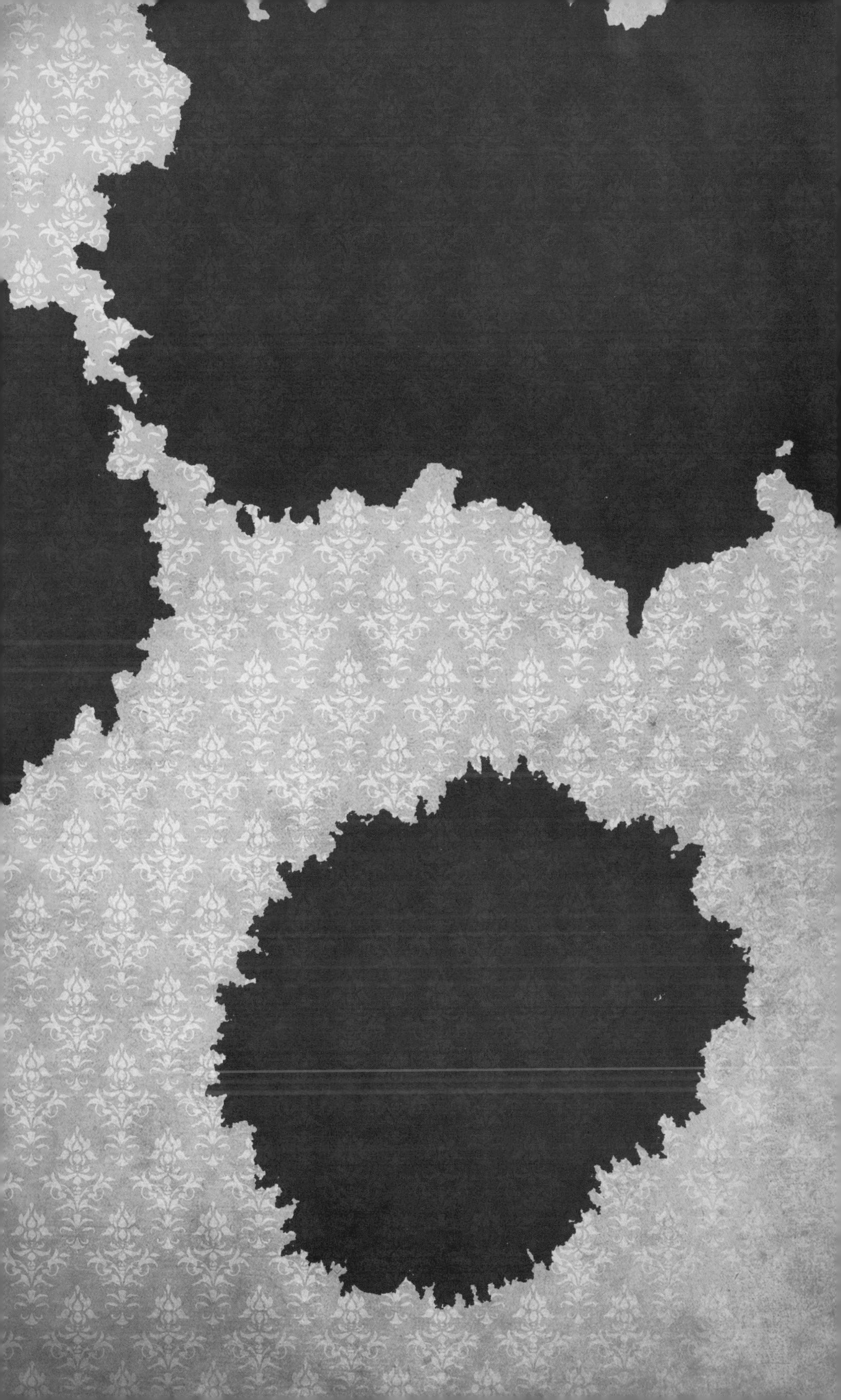

A STUDY IN EMERALD

SKETCHBOOK

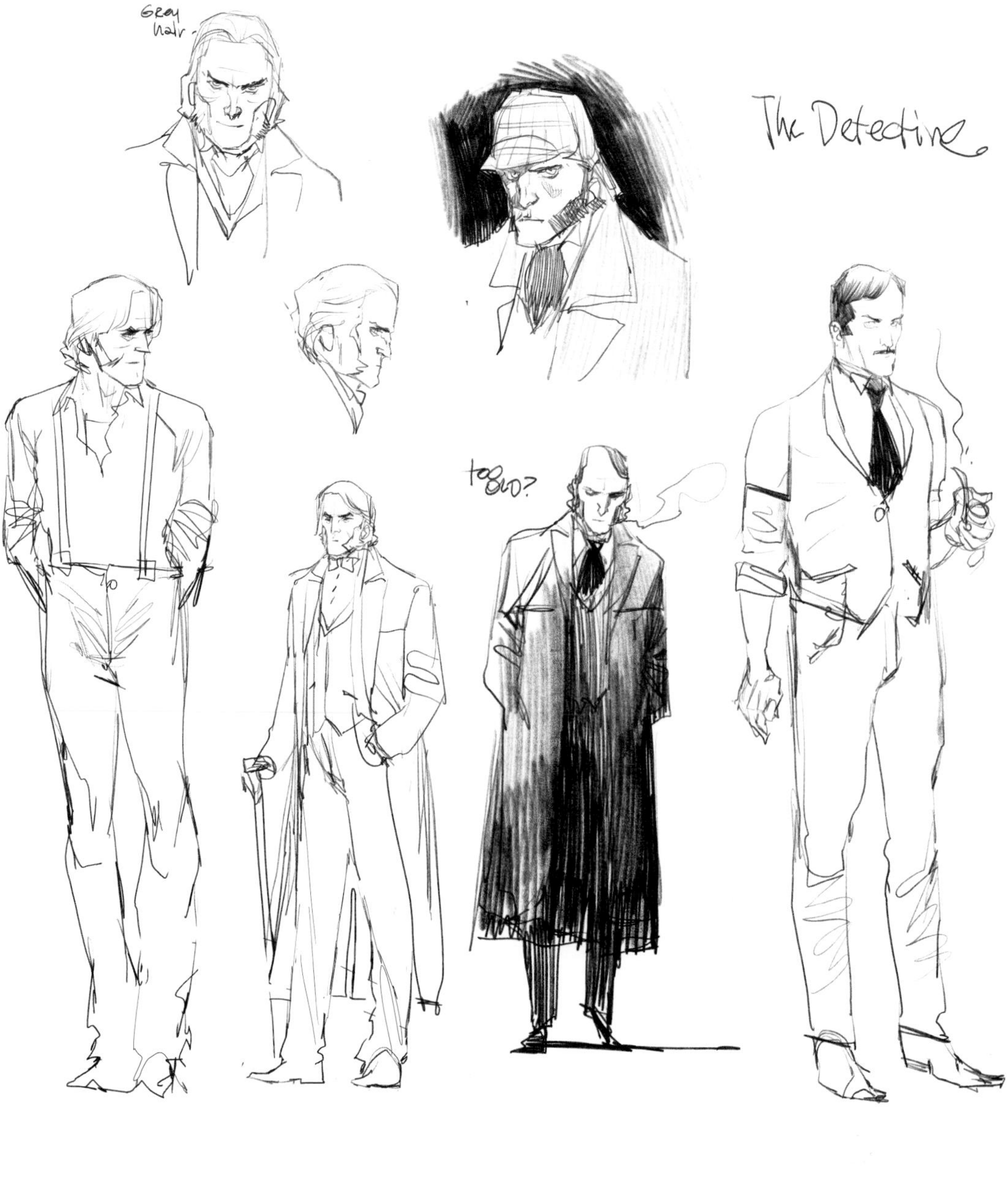

Grey hair.
The Detective.
too old?

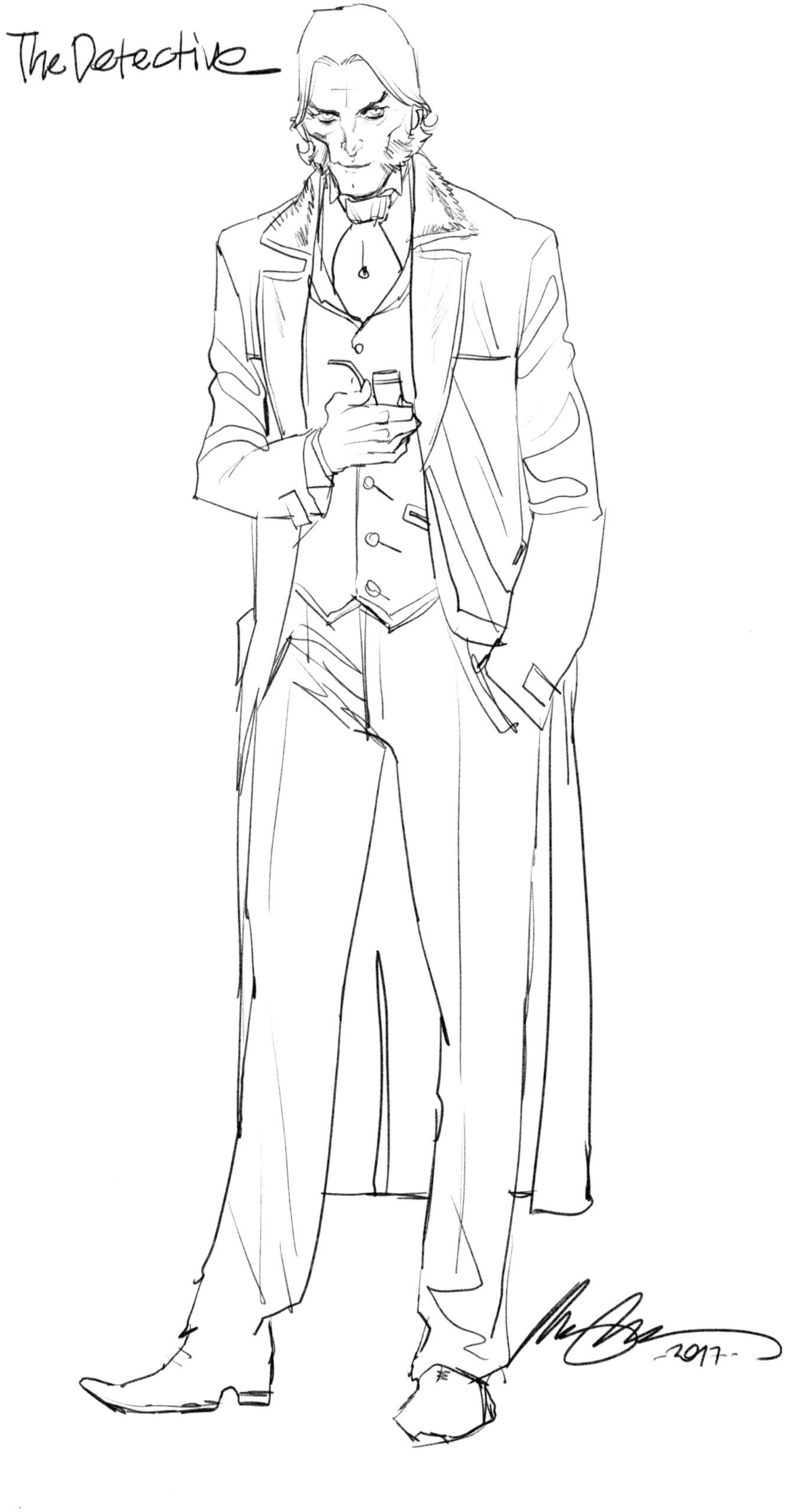
The Detective
2017

Early designs by Rafael Albuquerque for our mysterious protagonist—The Detective.

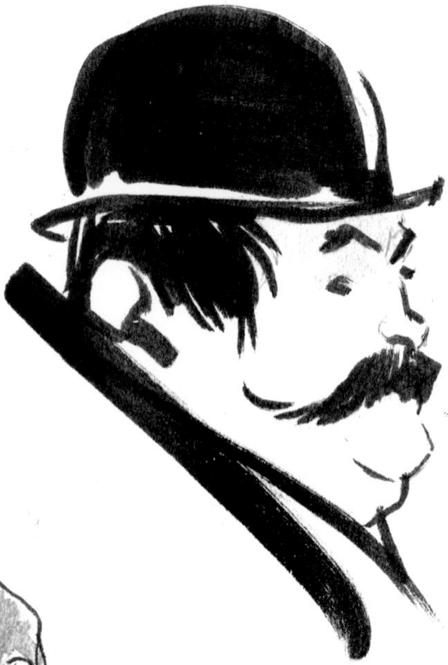

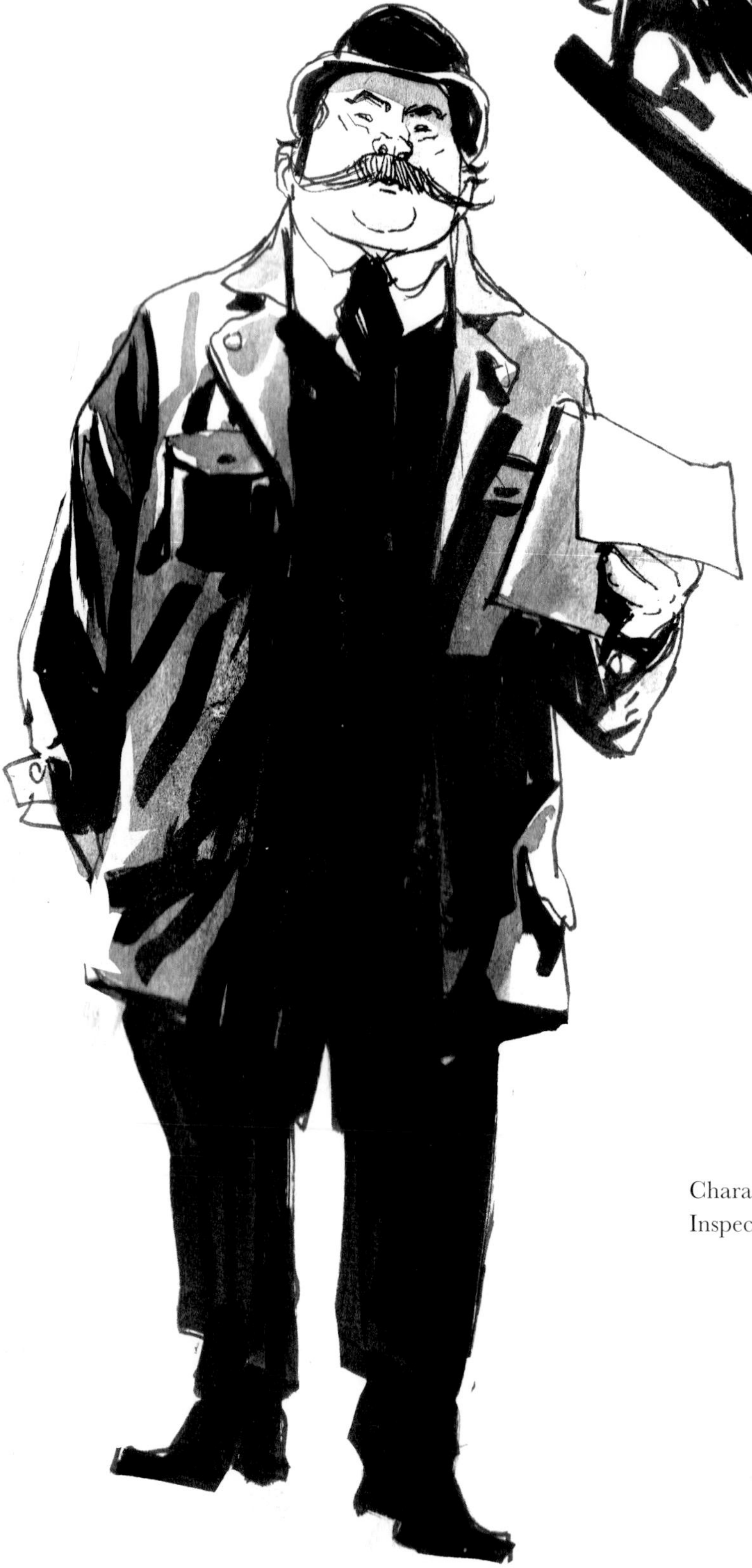

Character designs for
Inspector Lestrade.

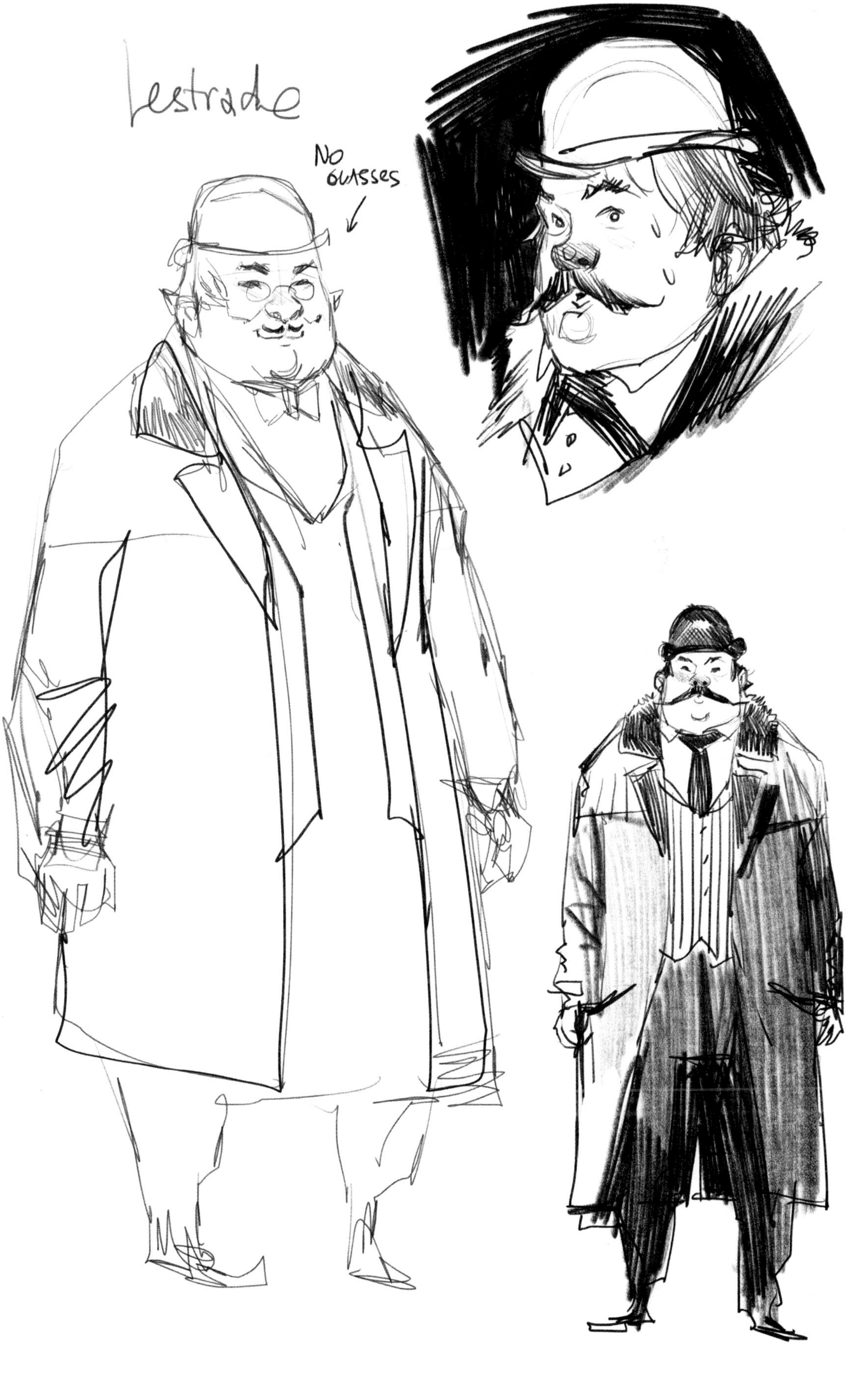
Lestrade
No glasses

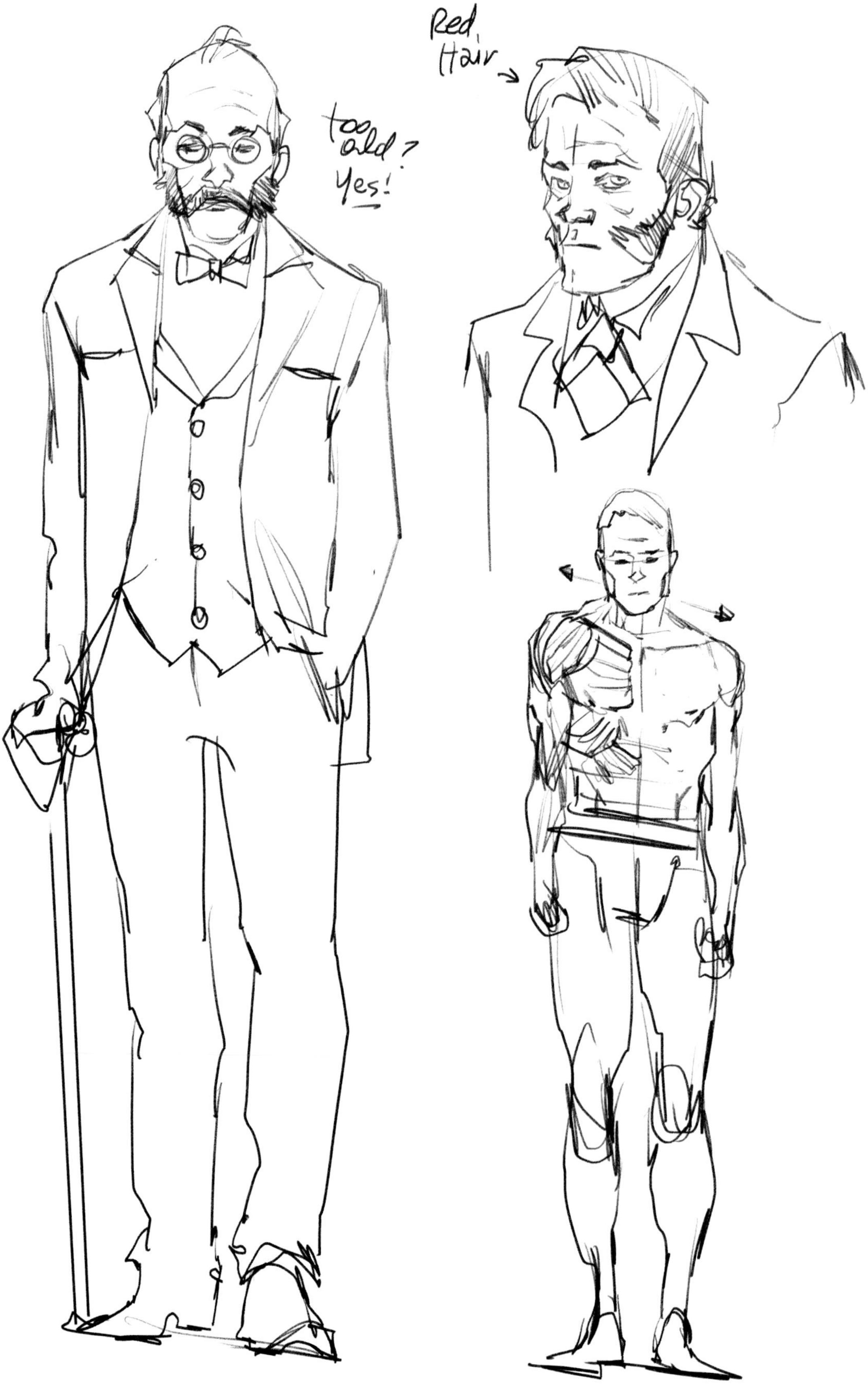
too old? Yes!
Red Hair

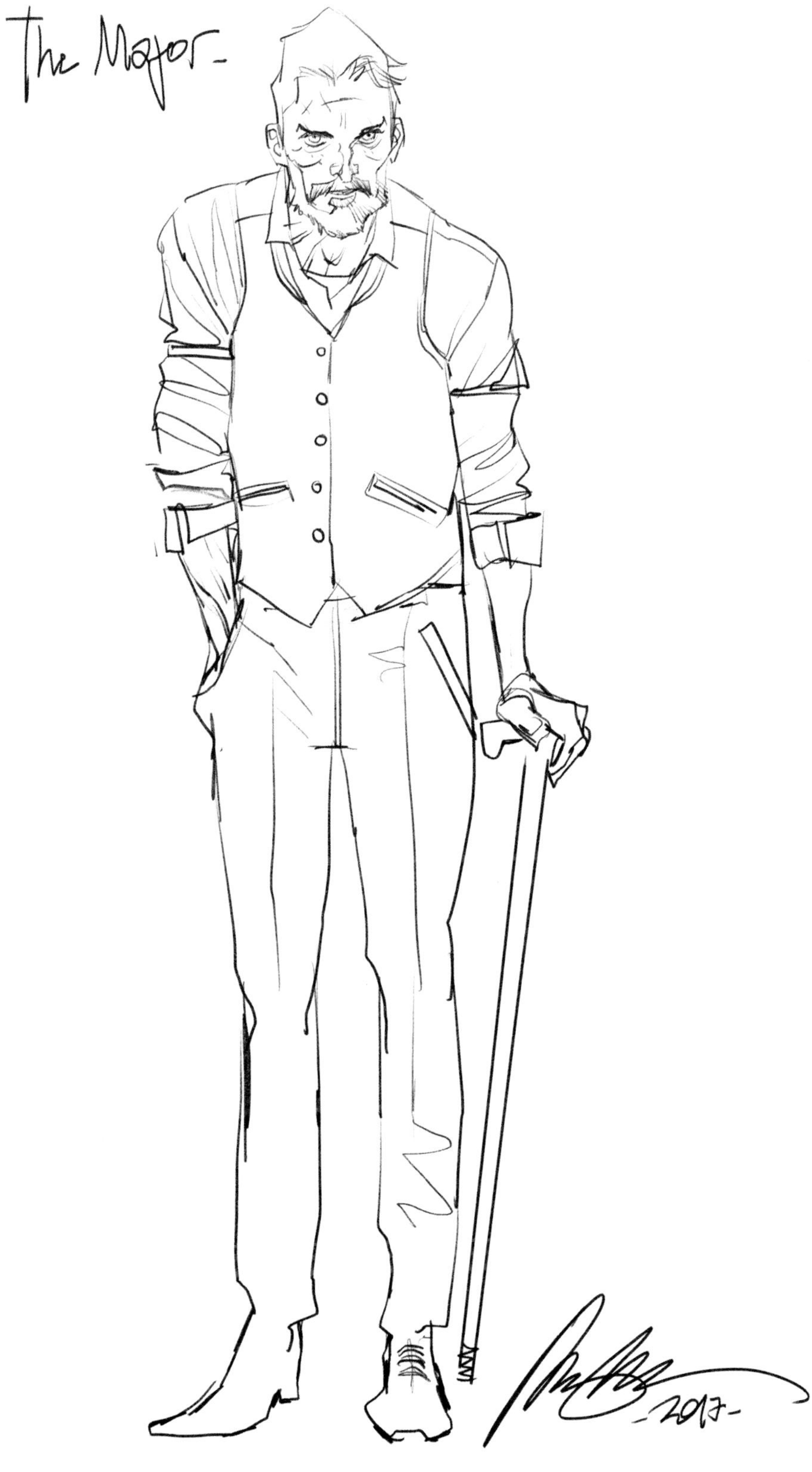
The Major-
-2017-

Several early character designs for the Detective's assistant—the Major.

The Major.

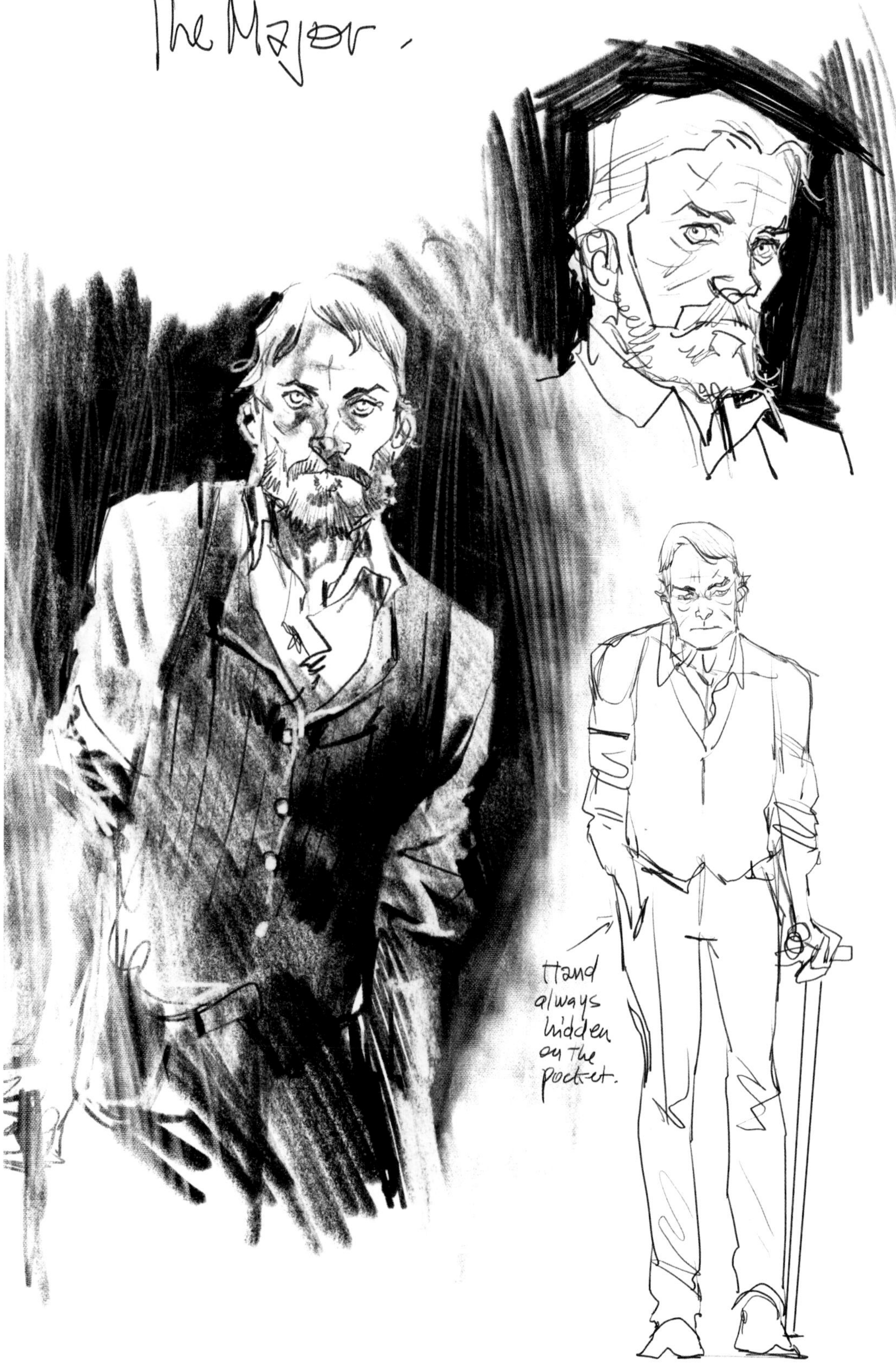
Hand
always
hidden
on the
pocket.

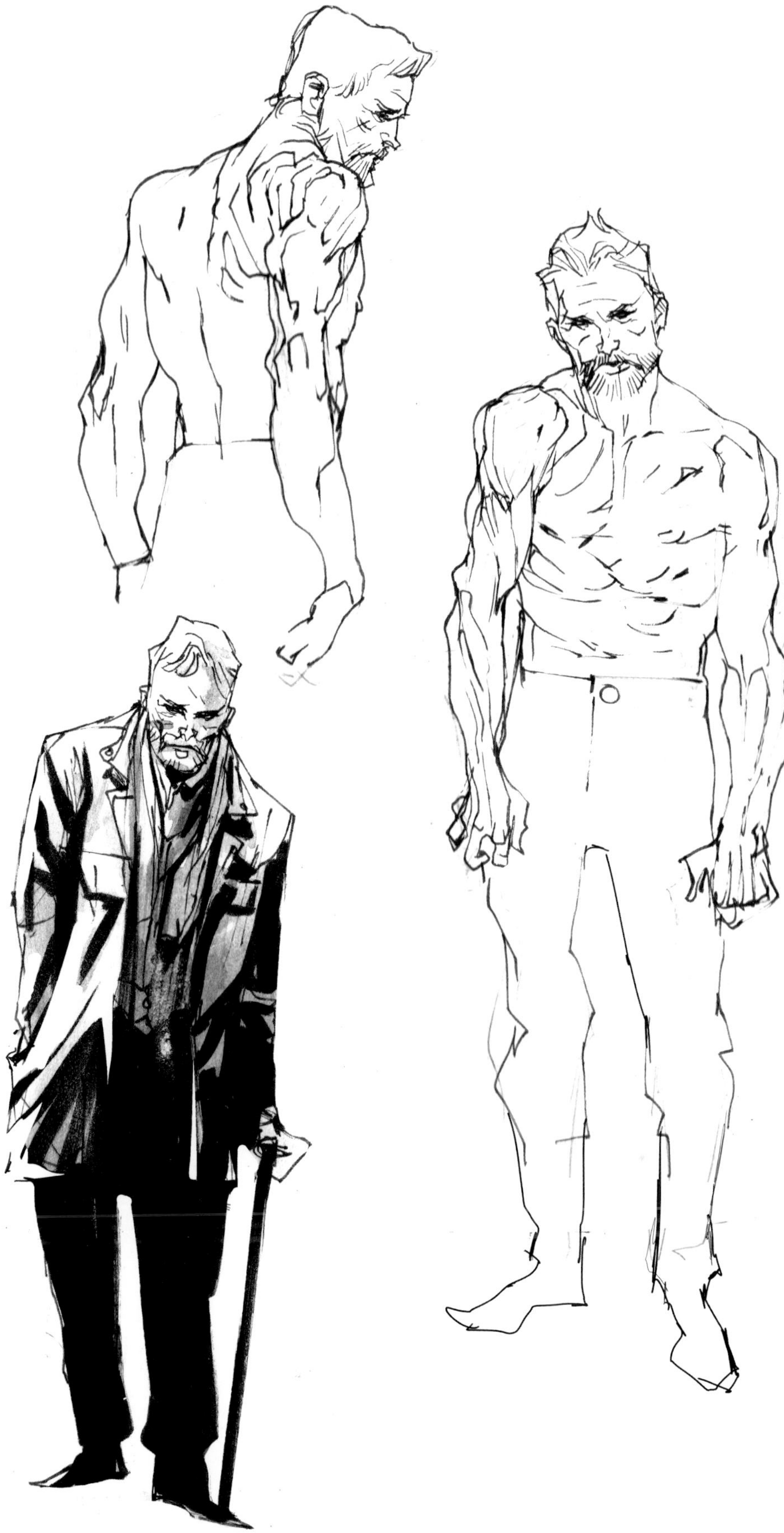

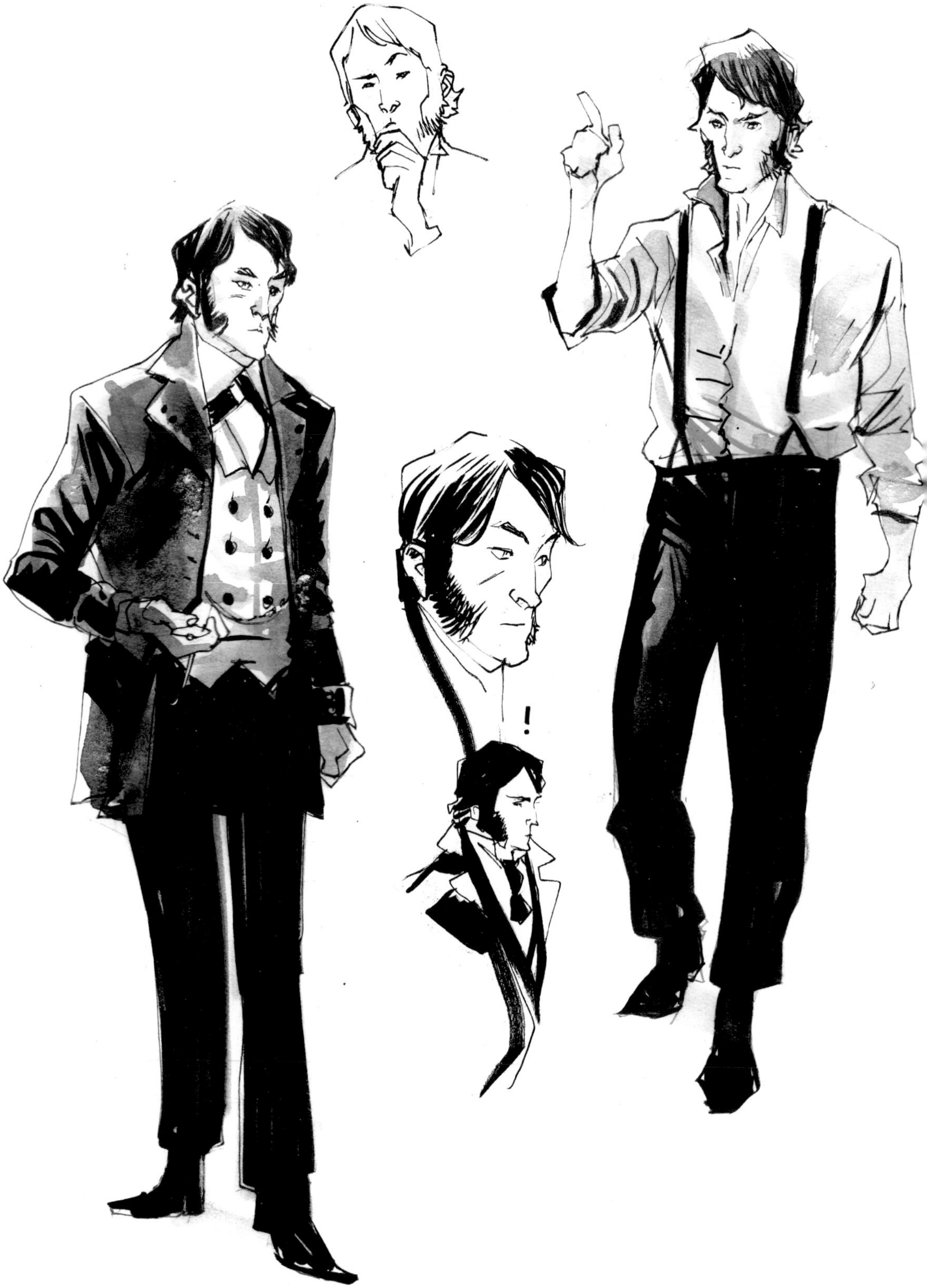
!

Designs for Vernet and our Lovecraftian Queen Victoria.

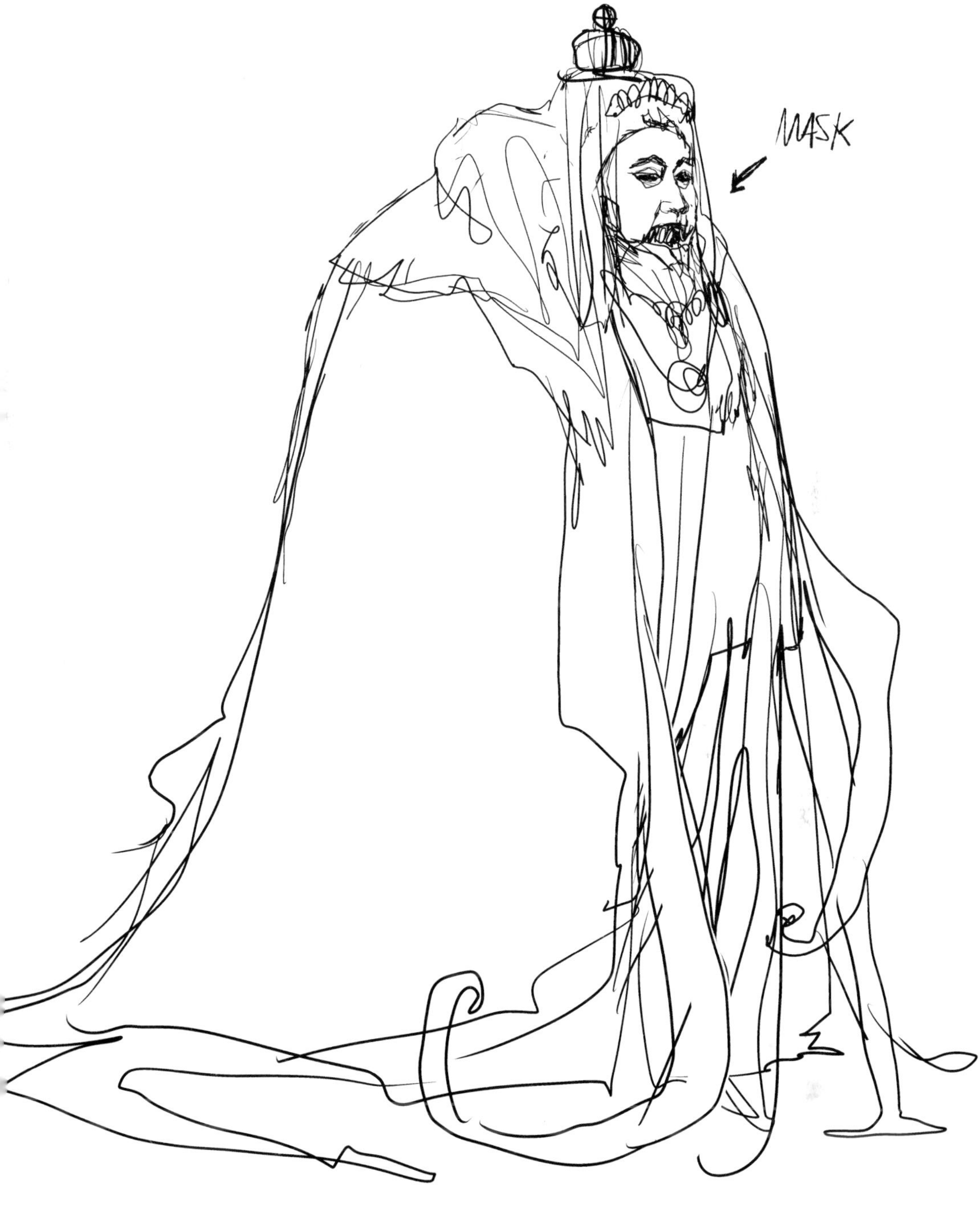
MASK